TINA AND THE BLUE BEAR
A SOLO MOTORCYCLE JOURNEY AROUND THE WORLD

PAUL EMERY, IS A BRITISH ADVENTURER, WRITER AND SPEAKER BASED IN BROOKLYN, NEW YORK. HIS EXPLOITS HAVE BEEN TESTED SAILING SOLO IN THE ATLANTIC, CLIMBING THE MOST TECHNICAL AND HIGHEST PEAKS IN EUROPE, FLYING WITH THE ROYAL AIR FORCE AND CYCLING ACROSS CONTINENTS ALL IN THE NAME OF WHAT PAUL TITLES 'A CURIOUS WANDERING TO UNDERSTAND THE WORLD WE LIVE IN'. FROM DODGING MINE FIELDS IN THE WEST BANK TO SPENDING TIME IN JAIL IN KAZAKHSTAN, HE ADMITS THAT THE ADVENTURES HAVE NOT ALWAYS GONE TO PLAN BUT AS HE BELIEVES 'WHEN THINGS GO WRONG THE ADVENTURE BEGINS'.

TINA AND THE BLUE BEAR

A SOLO MOTORCYCLE JOURNEY AROUND THE WORLD

BY PAUL EMERY

Copyright © 2016 by Paul Emery

Published by: Ellio Co

ISBN-13: 978-0692772331

First Print: September 2016

All rights reserved.

Cover design, texts, illustrations and photography: copyright © 2016 by Paul Emery

For Libby-

My sweetheart, for now and always

Table of Contents

TABLE OF CONTENTS	5
BOSTON	6
WASHINGTON	13
WEST VIRGINIA	25
PREPARING TINA	31
TENNESSEE AND FRIENDS	37
SEATTLE	72
VANCOUVER	78
SEOUL	88
SEA OF JAPAN	98
FAR EASTERN RUSSIA	102
MONGOLIA	162
THE ALTAI	187
KAZAKHSTAN	190
RUSSIA...THIRD TIME LUCKY	202
UKRAINE	205
SLOVENIA	221
CZECH REPUBLIC	222
GERMANY	225
BELGIUM	228
FRANCE	235
ENGLAND	239
HOME	243
EPILOGUE	247

BOSTON

I was on a street in south Boston, it was a small street only giving access to my building but it was a named street none the less, walking back across the grey tarmac to get the last of my bags, I hung my head low on to my chest, I was consumed with focus on the days ahead. I tried to recall what the road was called, maybe I never knew.

The hard work during the last year, running pens overs maps was now coming to a close, I could grasp the maps, tools, and suspension firmly under my bloodied knuckles yet now as this day unfurled beneath me, my grip was being folded back, breaking the tendons and tissues, I held only my thoughts.

I couldn't control the road ahead like I had controlled the packing, the bike building, the ticket buying, and route planning. I stood in the street, my feet in the thick wool socks felt warm and comforting with the braces of my trousers letting me know I was doing something fun. I stared at the empty spaces where once leaves held on but had run scared from the trees due to the thumping of snow and the wind all but barely gone, the air was crisp on my tongue. A blue breasted bird sat screaming some awful morning tune above me on a power cable, then the world fell silent.

Oh, fuck. What have I done? I'm going to puke. This had been a dream for so long and dreamers often lie. I took a few big breaths and made my way back to the apartment.

Drumming the beat to a Jackson 5 number I completed the packing of my bike, a ride a week earlier with all the kit had convinced me the loading configuration was correct. I was wrong, the fact was I'd never get it perfect, but my planning screamed for excellence. Now the result of all this work and turmoil was about to happen, I was numb, narrowed vision and expressionless. Opposite the garage of posh tanks of wealthy Bostonians sat my good time girl, grinning at me in the sunshine, coiled and willing.

The only other overnight trip I'd ever done with my bike, or any motorbike, was six hours after I bought her. Instead of heading home to London, I'd turned south and headed for the English Channel, I had nothing but my leather jacket and my new helmet but the freedom that the bike screamed was overwhelming. I got a cheap ferry ticket and headed for the centre of Paris, ducking, running and chasing the French cars, jumping the bike up onto paths as I couldn't find a way through the convoluted one-way system. I parked her in a hidden spot, safe and away from most lines of sight, I was cold down the left of my body, my tattered jeans had yielded in the first round against the biker's foe of the wind, spray, and the cold. The high exhaust that ran the inside of my right thigh kept a dichotomy across my skeleton. My dad's old leather jacket covered in blade marks and drink barely covered my long ape arms but the fit was oppressive enough to keep my heart and lungs warm.

My white helmet became a bracelet on my arm as I walked up the Rue Lepic and onto Rue Burq where I found a hidden tree lined square. I sank into a weakening wooden bench and locked my fingers behind my head, some Parisian bums around me slept, they were coated in dark greens and browns that had once been happy yellows and energetic blues, their decay brought them close to their surroundings. I was vibrating with the world; I had disappeared into her gaze.

    I swam in ideas for my Triumph and Me, where we could go and what we could learn, she wasn't the fastest, and had no protection from the elements but she was mine, and one day we would fade into the surroundings brought on by our wanderings, folding seamlessly into the truth of the world. The sun was disappearing behind beautiful buildings of stone and shape and mastery, as I watched the fusion reactor fold effortlessly into the Earth's shoulder. Not knowing where I was going to stay, I walked, humming, holding my heart aloft, turn, turn, turn, marching on.

    I found myself at a hostel upstream of the Moulin Rouge, it was above a fast food place, which caused a saturation of my walls with grease, the room was small and adequate. Above me, an impassioned couple nailed their love shut. To counter the smell, and to drown the drumming sounds, I opened the frail wooden window overlooking a narrow cobbled street. I sat on the flaky sill of my window and fell in love with women walking by, I dreamt of drifting down from my perch like a leaf into their hearts, overflowing their thoughts with my wanderings, the beautiful places I could take them, of course on the back of my motorcycle.

    The next morning, I had to push the bike to a petrol station. I'd run out of petrol just after firing up the bike. I had yet to learn the distance of a tank, so I devised a way using the trip to estimate when I needed to feed her. No petrol gauge only made me smile harder, down to the bone. After feeding her I stood in a cafe shooting strong coffee into my veins, I bought a croissant but folded it in a napkin and stored it in my pocket for later.

I had to work the following day, so I started the ride home. About two hours in I became tired and started to slump on my bars, straining to keep my eyelids open. I found a soft mound of grass a few turns from the main roads and I slept for a short while on the ground, pulling my jacket over my head and warming my back with the clutch cover. I recovered my energy and rode on.

I was free back then. Not now. I was encumbered with expectations and bags.

Kneeling down beside my bike, I whispered. 'Do you think we'll make it?'

'Sure we will,' she said

'Thanks, I'll look out for you if you'll do the same?'

'Always,' she said. 'Now don't question me again.'

I walked back to my apartment to lock the door and to say goodbye to my girlfriend, she stood in the doorway, her hands hanging from her delicate shoulders, all olive skin, thin fingers and beautiful curves, her deep brown hair had stuck to her face due to the goodbye tears. I hadn't dug runaways deep enough for what was coming out, yet down in the darkness, something had grown and oozed and clenched at us, a swarming wave of chemicals had eased us into the abyss. Ah shit, I was truly in love with her. She had swum with her eyes open and looked back at me knowing the route we'd taken, I, on the other hand, was clueless, ignorant by choice until this euphoria of motion sickness washed over me.

I'd said in every clichéd way I'd never be here again, saying goodbye to a girl I cared so much for, just like I had in London. Every other time the scales weren't in my favour but now the look on her face was similar to mine. I'd come to Boston after a seven-year relationship ending, people were married for less time and we had parted with little more than a "see you around". Back then I knew it was the right thing to do, our connection was one of comfort and ease rather than love & friendship. Libby and I were different, something I hadn't felt before, more stable and resistant, we were moored in the harbour, the sun was rising and we were looking forward to travelling to the next sunset together, so why the hell was I choosing to say goodbye? I'd screwed this up.

I was heading out solo, to ride a motorcycle around the world, to find the simple truth of adventure, me and the dirt of Mother Earth. Yet from where I had sailed, this simple, roaring lighthouse was ignored and I crashed nonchalantly into the hidden rocks. This was my first truth, a deep and raw one and I was leaving it behind.

'I'm going to miss you more than I thought,' I said.

'More than you thought?' Libby questioned.

'Well, I hadn't thought a thing about it til' now. Waypoints and emergency beacons were my thoughts.'

She looked perplexed.

'I really love you,' I mumbled

'I love you too.' She said, with a gentle smile that filled her face.
I held her hand.
'Hello.'
'Hi'
'If we get through this...'
'Just be safe.' She said
'I will, Tina said she will look out for me.'

I felt blind, somehow the stronger the light of love the more I pulled away, I had huge trust issues for as long as I could remember, being let down again and again by people close to me or who I looked up to, I knew this kept me insular but now it seemed to stop me from seeing what was good for me. I was angry and exhausted before I'd even turned the key in the ignition.

My wheels started turning at 10 a.m. on 1st April, the Boston roads were broken from the beating of overweight trucks and mountain tires, trees placed in perfected lines by the city planning authority directed me to where I was to say goodbye to my American family, surrogates that had climbed mountains and dived into streams, ran and laughed with me. They stood on the kerb and posed for a picture, it was time to roll on.

Tina was heavy and cumbersome, she utilized a design from the 60's, akin to Steve McQueen's bike in the Great Escape, with all the dense and heavy materials man has to offer, in the city streets she is a beautiful piece of British design yet using her as an adventure bike was ridiculous. I couldn't remember when I'd started naming my bikes, but each one had a name, this one was Tina, just like Tina Turner, she was made with a fantastic set of pipes.

I was extremely hot under my Siberia ready clothing, the bike reared under the weight, steering was a privilege I was yet to earn. I didn't even have the extra fuel tanks filled. Aggressive morning traffic eager to hide in their offices and shops kept bullying me, I screamed in my helmet not realising I was sat at some lights, pedestrians stopped to look for the source of pain, I smiled back. They stared not knowing what I was doing, I had no graphics or stickers, no banners or instructions leaflets to hand out on why I had loaded my bike to the hilt with bags, boxes, jerry cans, gizmos, and defensiveness. I needn't tell them why I was here or what I was trying to do, I knew what was what and I wanted it that way, and that was good enough, just tell everyone inside this white helmet and keep rolling.

I turned south and with my home behind me and the world below me. I jibed towards New York City, I didn't want to go in, just to ride by and wave.

'I'll see you in six months,' I screamed flipping the bird with a smile as I crossed the dirty George Washington Bridge.

I brawled along the New Jersey turnpike, just rolling into the unknown, signs for DC and beyond hung over me, twisting the throttle I blasted and the twin engine barked. The sun was fading, night rolling in, the temperatures dropping.

WASHINGTON

Instantly forgotten grey and white brick homes lined every street of Fairfax, Virginia, only to be interrupted by a McDonalds or a Dunkin Donuts, the night was cold as stars sparkled over an unquilted earth. I'd learned the weight of the bike and it grew more familiar, more tangible and more together. My days of filtering the boiling molecules of city traffic were firmly behind me, now I rode a behemoth on broad open roads to nowhere. It had rained quite a bit in the last few hours but my layers had kept me enclosed.

I swung into a poorly lit street. Spinning forward, my body wanted me inside, I wanted food, preferably warm and some fluids, hopefully some tea.

I knocked on the door with the four-digit house number I had memorised, the knocks jumped through the house, up and down the floors. I stepped backwards into the silent street, looking up at the structure, no lights shone outwards, the blinds were open, the whole street looked closed for business, no travellers here today, probably not tomorrow either.

The cold was getting through being carried by the tiredness of the day's miles. I opened my notebook to check the address, the light coming from a street lamp fifty meters upwind helped show me I was correctly placed. I found the number of my host and tapped it into my phone. My thoughts shifted, I wanted in, what if he didn't answer. What if this was an April fool's joke from my American family, slapstick and stupid, I was nine years old again having a wee in the dark on a camping trip, I was going to be eaten by a hideous monster all because of this joke. He answered.

'I thought you were coming tomorrow night?'

'No, I'm outside now.'

'I'll be back at 1a.m., I'm having dinner,' he shorted

'I'll get a motel, not to worry.'

Tears of anger and loneliness sat in my duct, aimed and ready. I couldn't afford too many nights in a motel, but my soul was burning out, the street darkened and the air was getting colder.

'No just wait.'

Maybe it was just his natural tone, I'd never spoken to the guy other than by email. He was good friend of a friend and offered to put me up as he happened to live on my route.

'Any ideas on where to wait?'

'McDonalds around the corner, twenty-four hours I think.'

'Ok.'

The street had two exits, one to this twenty-four-hour burger joint and the other to a motel. I decided a coffee and late night burger would be ok.

I got a message to saying he'd be home at 12:30. I headed over, he showed up at 1.

'Shall I pull the bike into the garage?'

'No space in there I'm afraid.'

'Ok, I do need to take off some essentials, though.'

'Ok.'

He stepped back to get a view of what I needed to do. The streetlight lit him up, his frame was stocky and I towered over him by a solid foot, his face was small and puckered, the total opposite to what was conjured over the phone. As he stood watching me, straight faced and cold. I started what would become a part of every day.

Keys.

Fuel tap.

Steering lock.

Unplug phone and battery charger.

Cover plug.

Three clips for the tank bag.

Secure the clips.

Fuel lock.

Webbing off.

Spare tires off.

Bungee straps unclipped.

Yellow bag.

Black bag.

Tighten loose straps.

Take the keys out the ignition.

'I'm done.'

'Cool, let me show you round.'

The garage opened into a well-equipped weights room.

'Just getting into weight training are you?' I pondered

'I have been for a while, I'm big into the bodybuilding scene.'

I had assumed by his small physique and muffin top he had just begun.

'Oh. Genetics plays such a huge part, you can try and try,' I pampered

'I'm struggling to find the right protein.'

'Yeah, that must be it.' I nodded.

I was in the warmth of four walls. What a marvel. He showed me around his big screen TV house, one of the American dreams, thick carpets felt like clouds under my thawing toes. Split over four floors this place was huge for one man, even five, bigger than I'd ever slept in, modern in that reused mould kind of way. I had my own room and my own bed. I grinned and passed out.

I awoke in melancholy, reflecting on my first day and I felt ashamed and still exhausted of the emotions. It was my first day and I was ready to walk away and leave it all behind, go back to the truth I'd found in Libby, my girl. The love I was holding, let it out and sink into the summer with her and the waves of the Atlantic, start building our home together, wherever it may be. The savings I had put together for this trip could put us close to a home, we wanted to build our own on a plot of land, exactly to our specs, where did my decisions all go wrong? I felt doomed to constantly choose the wrong path. I was never going to find a place to call home if I kept running away.

I wandered out the garage door looking up and down the street, it didn't seem so menacing now, and I knew the whole story of this street, told in honesty by the sun. I had wanted to visit DC for a while, the capital district of the country I had called home for the last eighteen months. Politics in America was the epitome of a dichotomy, they rue the underdog, which is a beautiful piss in the face of Etonian wink wink nudge nudge British tripe, yet what makes the majority of their pack is a crazy bunch, caricatured from wonders of absurdity.

The buildings and monuments were pretty and elegant and they definitely knew how to remember a fallen soldier. I parked and bumbled around the streets, looping around the grand avenues and promenades, all littered with keen parents educating their children, miserable suits and old folk not quite sure on their location. I finally looped back to Tina, I had repurposed an instruction manual holder from a tractor to hold my tool roll, it kept the grease and oil from my food and clothes. but it had snapped away from its fixings due to the weight, nothing some zip ties couldn't fix.

With the fix in place I continued my wanderings up a hill for about half a mile to get some lunch from a burgundy sandwich shop on the ground floor of a grand imperial building, hand built from stone and glass, I sat with my worked hands and wild hair amongst the office gossips social that happened here every weekday at lunchtime. I finished the sandwich and soup and chose another direction to walk, heading off for another part of DC.

I ended up in Georgetown, slick kids skated by yummy mummy's strolling their future honour students. Everyone was smiling at me, I smiled back. I walked into a record shop to replace my headphones that that morning I had managed to melt onto my exhaust, walking back out of the shop through their black wooden door, I craned my neck skywards as the sun wilfully shone on my thoughts and settled me down for an hour of rest against a tall hardwood tree in a nearby park, with my ankles crossed and the dirt cupping my arse, I just glided amongst my thoughts and chuckled, I was going round the world, a bum of mother nature, a hobo of planet earth, it was psychedelic.

The road was a straight shot back to the house. With no luggage on-board other than me and my music. I blasted a tonne all the way. Untouchable. The sun shone, having no alternative, on everything that was new that day.

'There may be a shot of rain, just wait for the warmth,' I said in my helmet.

That night the host and I connected, we found a mutual love of pizza, justifying the gluttony by the potential of the cold days ahead, probability said there had to be at least two months out of the four which would be bad, in Siberia the winter arrived late, she kept coughing out some minus 20s and plenty of snow still lay around.

Over the slices of pizza, the good vibrations were helping me relax. The animosity was all me, people could more readily believe in a person's smile and happiness than they could in their unjustified sorrow. I learnt he was a gentle kid with a soft talk and as he spoke the all too common truth arose that he was as lost as I was, unjustified in the only road he'd known, when will men drop these compasses they hoped would point to salvation? The giddy blackness of uncertainty is so sweet, we just need to lean forward and lick it, sink our teeth in and show our blackened gums.

I had become tired of the mornings that had repeated themselves over the last five years, a coffee would be sat in my left hand; my right hand rubbed the left nook of my nose giving my brain cells time to align like soldiers on parade. It would be another day spent at war. A battle for the senses, for today I will see the perfect female form, endless horizons, and lost cities, we just have to trust that all these places are real, just not to me and probably not to you.

Why are we so content with the streams of imagery, single quips and shaky footage of sun flared wanderings to sculpt our lives that claim to offer the answer or even inspire it? The only thing these truly give us is tiredness. A weary set of eyes to see the bastardization of the world we care so much for, yet know so little about. This age of worry makes it is easy to hide behind screen and page. If we were to step out, smash the polarised lenses, walk until our feet were crippled, would we then become a mad one, one who understands the world and all its beauty and have our own, irremovable images that you simply cannot question.

As a child, I was lost in worlds of great adventure, hardship, and determination sculpted by Willard Price, Joey Dunlop, Ranulph Fiennes, Mallory, Scott, Sheene and the publicity exploits of Richard Branson, yet that sense of adventure was still to be mine.

My primary school brothers, Miles and Paul Colgrave, lived and worked on a grand, stone built farm not more than a mile or two up the hill from my Grandparents. My parents' house was a further five miles down the road. I awoke every morning in the desolate main town, a few hundred meters up from a big factory chugging out smells across the rows of 1950s houses, where the dirty dish water stayed and lingered.

On hot days the acrid smell of the industry passed down by the rivers and winds would ooze from the walls, down the gutters and into the alleyways, when the smell got too strong I would run, grab my green BMX and pedal as fast as my lungs would take me all the way to Miles and Paul's house. The air was clean and rich there, I would stay until the sun disappeared then would have to ride the fields and alleyways back home.

Out on their farm I learned how to aid in the birth of lambs, drive tractors, move hay bails, catch rats during harvest and build crossbows, it didn't take many hours til' I learned to love and seek the discomfort of the outdoors. During those days, embers were lit.

The first time I truly got away on an adventure all of my own was to South Africa, all to see a girl. I was 16 and madly in love. She lived for the majority of the time with her mother, in a small village near my home town of Banbury, each summer she would leave and head towards South Africa. Where she spent her summers with her authoritarian father, who was a retired banker of some note and now lived alone with a cook, two gardeners and a handyman, all in a grand house not far from Cape Town. The idea of spending a summer apart was too much to comprehend so we devised a plan I would fly out and stay with her and her Dad for a few weeks, all I needed was the OK from the authorities, I was able to convince my parents her father had invited me because my girl's parents never spoke.

On the flight over I was bumped up to first class by the airline, a way to keep a better eye on me I suppose, attention that wasn't unfamiliar. To kill time, a vicarious businessman challenged me to cram as many blankets into our carry-on luggage as possible, my old school backpack could only hold two but we were pleased with the six we got into his briefcase.

With my backpack full, I left the airport and hitched a ride with a local called Jurie; although humble in stature his hands told of a life full of hard graft. Jurie and I had only one thing in common, we were going in the same direction but I felt at total ease with him, curious of the stories he held. Lying in the bed of his truck I dreamt of my girl's hourglass body and the adventure I was on, the clouds seemed to spell out my thoughts in brail across the sky with the warm air pushing a plethora of feelings deep within my skin.

I left my new friend at a set of crossroads all leading to what seemed to be nowhere, relying on the trust of a person I'd just met. The truck merged into the heat shaken horizon leaving me to guess the route to my one true love. Stood opposite me in a recently painted white and green bus stop was a tall and slender lady contemplating my behaviour, like a therapist towards an abused child. In simple and elegant clothes, she stepped forward, out from the shade of the hut where she proceeded to beckon me over.

I walked to her side hoping to receive assistance, she placed her hand on my shoulder like a teacher tired of sending me to detention, bending down she said, with the utmost sincerity, "Riding in vehicles with black people is a true risk to your safety." Feeling the awkwardness flood my cheeks, I decided which road to go down, I acknowledged her advice to make the situation end and then paced quickly down the sand and grit road, making sure I didn't look back.

Number 25, there it was, I'd actually made it half way around the world to a small coastal village east of Cape Town, all for a girl. I was grinning from ear-to-ear, hoping my efforts would let me go all the way. My enthusiastic hopes, however, were soon extinguished at the door as a confused grey haired man that answered soon realised I wasn't there to see him. I remained on the porch as I listened to the loud, one-sided constructive discussion going on inside that concluded I could stay but only in the outhouse, good job I had those extra blankets.

I spent two weeks that summer walking on beaches, making out and going down. I never did go all the way but I had opened my eyes for the first time to the world and it seemed to be looking back. I felt so removed and far away yet totally at home in my strange new surroundings.

Arriving back in England ready to start my A-Levels, I was left with stories to tell, blank pages to fill and ideas to contemplate. Not long after my return my one true love dumped me due to a new lad in town who owned a brand new Renault Clio 16v in race blue. Unable to compete with a French hot hatch and heartbroken, I fumbled through my exams and longed to get away, I soon headed east to Borneo to teach English in a remote village some four days by aircraft and foot from the nearest town.

I did adventures here and there but I longed to do something big and scary like Ranulph Fiennes had done when he went to the Poles. This desire sat in me like an unbalanced weight, giving me a sense that I had to always keep moving and if I didn't something bad would happen, I didn't know what that bad thing was, maybe it was a fear to be alone with just my thoughts but I was always on the go and a big expedition, like riding a motorcycle unsupported around the world on my own, might quell this urge, and help me find some peace and let me have my own stories to share, rather than basking in the light of others.

WEST VIRGINIA

After expelling the first day's fears amongst the statues and pizza boxes of DC I continued on the road south. Tina was flying high, the bright sun grew the land into the sky, with her stomach full of fuel I knew I could cut away and run loose through the hills, where America fought for its freedom.

The hills of Virginia were singing to themselves this morning, I was awake and on the bike for 6 a.m. I was there in time to hear their song, every morning nature sang when the sun folded into the sky, you just had to fight the weight of your eyes to be there to hear it, every day before this one I had lost the fight, going down before the first round bell rang, I had received backhanders from my soft pillows and the gentle pair of eyes staring at me each morning. Now this window view through the plastic glass of my visor was my sanctuary and offered me an uninterrupted view of Virginia.

I parked where the sealed tarmac turned to lose gravel and sat down on crooked stones hanging above a steep drop down into a spring green valley, the trees, and mounds, cops and tracks rose and fell on the waves of earth running away beneath me. Easy hymns of the morning dew and swooping birds sung together whilst holding hands, peace was deep within me, a serenity not to question, its fragility lay like the silk of a web.

I rode on the blue ridge highway for another hundred miles dancing the bike like a pendulum along the path cut by man through the face of this hillside, the road was smooth grey with the steep cut stone to my left crowned in hickory and oak, the oxygen they expelled fell down across the road and to the valley floor below my brake pedal. Swaying me further and further, skipping the bike down this foreign road in the glory of a beautiful morning was utter bliss.

I rode for a good sixty miles without seeing another beast walking on two legs, just some feathered fellows upon the rising air and other little creatures too fast for my eye to see. There were 1000 roads to take south but I had this one and this one had me. As one hundred miles approached on my trip I looked for a petrol station to fill and had to head away from my river run in the sky, I cut east for a short while and rolled into a fuel station framed in old trees, they held back the heat of the sun forcing me to fill quickly and move on.

I hadn't eaten since yesterday evening, not for the want of food but the new epiphany that time had ceased to exist, therefore the need for food for my soul, my heart or my muscles was just not there. What a mad man I was becoming, this dirty starving beast traipsing across the planet. I was unencumbered by sanity until my spokes stopped spinning then like a wave from a North Sea storm, smashing against my back my airy arrogance of the day broke and I fell back down. Hunger set in and I would shovel any mere morsel that would be within arm's reach straight into my gut, again and again, until a heaviness set in, heavy in my stomach, my bones and eyelids.

Tonight's feed was some noodles I had bought for 50¢ from a Chinese supermarket in Boston, they had a cartoon kid on the packet with huge eyes and he had made me laugh. I planned to camp in the hills just outside of the town of Roanoke. I turned right and then left onto a single track road, as it continued to bend I ran past an old train signal box that was slowly being eaten by vines and weeds from the damp lush ground, ducking down and around a sharp bend I rode through rotten standing water in a small greasy tunnel under the tracks leading to a slip road. As I rolled from the darkness of the underpass, there sat stone built houses marking the end of the town and the start the tree covered road to the campsite, after another 400-mile day I was ready to pitch camp and lay back in the leaves with my burnt in dirt and crooked fingers and fall majestically asleep.

 I pulled up to a wooden barrier that was once red and white, the majority of the warning paint had been peeled back by the weather and now sat amongst the leaves and twigs, further back a rusted chain had been belted around two large meshed fences, above them spanned a plank of oak holding the remaining letters "ELCOM". I got off the bike and walked up to the fence, a handwritten notice covered in cellophane stated the campsite went out of business last summer and was not to reopen this season. I rolled my eyes to the sky, Virginia had about thirty minutes of light left to give, not enough time to find somewhere else. So I pushed through a hole in the fence and walked down the path in the green wood to where it bent into the undergrowth.

 On the right of the track sat a beige RV with mould growing over the tires and window sills, the dark blue curtains were drawn inside, it was slowly becoming part of the nature, it's inevitable step in its own evolution. A hiss came from a burner, ablaze on a broken paving slab near the door, I rolled forward onto my toes so I could lean over the pot and see what was inside, a red soup simmered away. I knocked. Life sprung to its feet in an amongst a clatter of pans and junk, I stepped back to allow for the door to open and out peered a man, bent at the waist, his face was not accustom to visitors. Dressed in blue shorts with an unbuttoned shirt that barely concealed his unfed frame.

'Hello,' I said.

'Hi.'

'Do you think I can camp here tonight?'

He looked both ways.

'How'd you get in here?'

'I came through the hole in the fence, I'm riding my motorcycle around the world, this is day three,' I blurted

He stepped down from the doorway and looked up the track to my bike.

'We get a few bikers come out here and camp'.

'You can go out back, away from any eyes, the authorities let me camp here you see so I make sure stuff like this don't happen.'

'You won't know I'm here.'

'Follow the road down and around to the left.'

He seemed harmless. I was grateful. I walked back to my bike, the evening air was warm and thick, like a rich coffee it helped me keep the tiredness of the day at bay. I pushed the bike through an opening in the fence and rode down past the RV, the road spiralled upwards around a small hill. I pulled into a spot that was covered with leaves and branches. I swept my foot left and right clearing the ground making sure it was good for the tent, the ground was covered with small gravel and sand, firm and dry. I walked back to the bike and splayed the pannier lids to give myself a big working area, I dug into my boxes and found my sleeping kit, I pitched the tent and unfolded my stove to get some food in before all the light was gone.

Darkness was chased in quickly by the dense canopy above, I had my sleeping bag in my hands when I heard the crushing of the dead leaves behind me, I turned to see the old man, he had moved all the way across the campground without a sound.

'You're going to have to go,' he said

'How come?'

'If, um… they find you here I will lose my lodgings.'

'Umm ok, it's getting late though man, I really don't know the area and it will be hard for me to find another place at this time of night.'

He fell silent.

'See the hut over there.' He pointed to a small brick shed that didn't have any discernible path to it some 500 meters back into the woods. 'If you camp behind there you'll be totally out of sight.'

His request seemed strange as I was already half a kilometre into a dense wood at the end of the shabby path, yet I didn't want this sad old hobo to be hiked out of here on my account so I obeyed.

The tent was lifted fully erected onto my bike, I then rode around to the back of the brick shed. The last few minutes of light went as I spilt out the last of the washing up water from my bowl and rolled back onto my sleeping bag. I fell asleep quickly although I felt a heaviness spinning in my gut brought on by the loneliness of this nest hidden almost a kilometre away from a road leading nowhere. I knew then I needed someone to harmonise with and scream into the night. My only friend called Thoughts was an absolute shit bag, he never shut up or spoke about something I didn't already know. Right now I was in self-imposed solitary confinement in this Virginia hillside, this hobo school I'd signed up to was tough. It was beating me down and it wanted to keep me there, but each time you joined a class it would whisper, *'When you get up from a lesson you'll be taller and stronger and more truthful.'* Maybe it was time to bunk school.

PREPARING TINA

The work prior to the trip took me almost a year. Overall I am not that disciplined, other than the fact I know I can move fast and become maniacal when I have an idea in my head. Once I had spoken of my plan to others I was imbued in my word, initially I felt nervous and overwhelmed, unsure whether I could physically, mentally or even financially afford it. It was a huge undertaking and after my initial pencil and paper brainstorming sessions it was clear there were a hundred other things that I could do with the money, time and effort.

I finally came to the decision on committing whilst at a friend's party. I was slightly boozed and like so many times before felt a need to overcompensate for some missing link, like lineage, wealth, title, job, as if any it actually mattered. I blurted to a whole bunch of friends that I had to leave the US because my Visa needed to be renewed and so I had decided to ride my motorcycle around the world. Maybe it was my casual tone of my voice but the room erupted with wows and amazement. I sobered instantly as questions of how, why, where and why and how and why and how flew my way. I tried to field them the best I can but the reality was I hadn't a clue how I was going to do it. Strangely though it seemed that a few of the group new intricately what I needed to do, how much it would cost and the route to take. They became authoritative on the subject. A heated discussion erupted, totally excluding me.

The following morning, I awoke with the standard hangover and my usual craving for bacon but this time I had this other feeling, this, 'Oh shit what have I done' feeling like when getting naked in front of people because it seemed like a good idea at the time, but this feeling although similar was deeper, my phone was lighting up, people still imbued by the adventure were texting me.

OK, it was now set, I was going out solo round the world on a motorcycle and like any great adventure from the Marco Polo to the Apollo space mission it all started with a spreadsheet, well maybe not Marco Polo but you get the drift. With a strong cup of coffee in hand I took to creating the largest brain dump I had ever done. What I thought would be a couple of key points led to an extensive spreadsheet covering kit, route, contact info, legal, visa requirements, bike upgrades, saving plan and a whole other set of miscellaneous items yet to be clarified and answered.

Soon the flood of delivery parcels, packages, and letters started arriving. My kitchen table turned into a world map and with a red pen I started circling the places I knew others had been, I soon realized my timeline of three months was very short, especially compared too others that had gone before me, such as Ted Simon, whose book had been given to me by my Uncle a few years back. Ted's stories of adventure struck a deep cord. His round the world motorcycle adventure lasted four years which seemed to be the norm. I couldn't afford to do that type of expedition and deep down the fear of being alone for so long scared me to the core. A reality was starting to dawn on me, I had realized early on I wanted more than what my hometown offered, but going where no one in my family had walked before meant a majority of the time I was on my own, not only in the moment but in reflection, and now I was realizing I wasn't as tough on my own as I let myself believe.

    I had to keep pushing through, I knew that if I stayed working hard and focused I would get to the finishing line. Maybe just maybe a little closer to the dream I often dreamt off. The large kitchen table in a farmhouse, with a flagstone floor, my wife, my children. I dreamt often of this home I wanted to make, sometimes bringing me to tears just thinking of it, the feeling of cold slate on bare feet, the feel of a warm dog's hair brushing by my leg, cooking eggs in one hand whilst holding one of my daughters on my hip as she told me about her wonderful dreams. Money was scarce growing up and it gripped silently to issues that came up in the family. We made do, but I knew that there was so much more out there, new horizons to explore and I wanted to try it. Somehow, through some means this adventure would get me closer to that dream.

    I had to stay focused, because of the time constraints I started to drastically amend my route. I thought I had my route set, then I learnt of a thing called a Carnet de Passages (CDP). A CDP is a document that is needed to enter and exit certain countries with expensive equipment like a motorcycle, and upon further examination I realized that the cost of the said document with three times the cost of my whole trip budget. I received quotes from fifty thousand dollars to over two hundred thousand. There were numerous roadblocks in the planning stage but this was a huge hit.

Trustworthy information pertaining to a non-CDP route was difficult to find. Everyone I spoke too talked in definite terms, either for a route existing or exclaiming point blank that a route never had or never will exist. It took a long and extensive sift through various country documentation to find that I could go from the US to Canada to South Korea to Russia to Mongolia back to Russia to Kazakhstan back to Russia again then to the Ukraine, Slovakia, Czech Republic, German, Belgium, France then England all without a CDP. Once confirmed, Libby and I went out to celebrate.

Next was the bike, Tina was parked on a side street, glistening in the summer sun. She was a blast to ride in the city, her wide bars dropped her into corners with ease, her high pipes terrified people walking as she backfired, the non-existent protection made you feel raw and tough but she was no adventure bike. The bike she was built to emulate weighed less than $1/100^{th}$ of what she did, she had about one hundred and ten miles in range and her suspension would bottom out at the slightest pothole, yet the cost of something else was out of the question, I simply couldn't afford it. So for better or worse it was Tina that had to carry my arse around the world but certain things had to change.

My first task was the wheels and suspension. I replaced the front fork inners with sealed cylinders and Ohlin's on the rear with separate reservoirs, and I had to put them on upside down to allow for the only pannier system I could find that would fit my bike. For the wheels I changed to all black sealed spokes, not only did they look mean as hell, they also allowed me to run both tubed and tubeless tires, just in case I had no other option. I took to fitting the tires onto the new rims in my lounge, cursing and bleeding into the night as I used the 'adventure-sized' tire levers to prise the tires into place. I had a nightmare removing the old springs from the original forks, resorting to taking them to the fire station workshop across the road and using their pneumatic tools.

    I installed a double jerry can bracket on the back of the bike to help overcome the range issues yet the weight once fully fuelled took some adjustment. For the wiring I installed a new lithium battery that reduced weight and gave a little amount of space to install a powered USB and GPS. For protection against the elements I installed a six-inch windshield, it took the brunt of a direct blast from my chest whilst keeping Tina's look, which of course was paramount for expedition success. Lastly, I changed the bulbs to the brightest most obnoxious ones I could find.

    The changes were all needed but on one of the few test rides I did between completing the bike and departing I found her very top-heavy, leaning quickly into corners, although with the new suspension she held firm and coped with the additional weight well.

    During this time, I had started acquiring all the kit needed to fill the panniers and bags, from lightweight tents and stoves, which could run on any flammable liquid to stickers that went on my helmet that said my blood type and contact information in various languages if I was be to found unconscious somewhere. I also had some stickers printed with my name and the Union Jack, like Colin McCrae had on his Subaru and put them all over my helmet. I upgraded my brown leather work boots to dedicated biker boots that clasped all the way up the calf. I pieced together a specific toolkit keeping only the tools, sockets and bolts that fitted Tina, everything else was to be left at home, the essential paracord for use as a washing line and to keep food off the ground, a compass, torch and some waterproof matches. Upfront I had a tank bag with waterproof copies of my route, first aid kit, emergency beacon, camera, spare batteries, snacks and goodies and a pair of sunnies. In my chest pocket would always sit my phone, wallet, and passport. Those would never leave my side, and if I had to make a run for it for whatever reason I would have the means to do so.

For my riding jacket and trousers, I had always used an all season two piece. I was nearly lured into buying some ridiculous adventure suit that could fly me to the moon and back but although my current suit was husky and well worn, it kept me warm and dry and I simply couldn't ask for more. The fabric had also proven to be easily repairable with gaffer tape.

With money sitting somewhere between tight and non-existent, I reached out to numerous companies looking for sponsorship, only to be asked, "Do you have a book or TV deal?". I struck lucky with a few giving me kit at wholesale but other than that it was just me and my savings.

TENNESSEE AND FRIENDS

I had been holding onto an invite I got from a farmer called Andy in Tennessee. He'd heard about my trip through my website and had emailed me directly, I had never heard of the guy before but rolled the dice and decided that I had to trust the unknown, it was what the trip was about, or so I hoped! He had offered shelter in one of his barns, it was a short way outside of Nashville, meaning I could spend more time the following day diggin' the blues of the penny bars and whistle back streets of this legendary heartbreak town that was to be my next stop. I couldn't wait to spin my tyres onwards.

The green roof of my tent lit up in the Virginia Hills at a dash past 4 a.m. My entire left flank was frozen from the ground, it was my prize for a restless sleep amongst the breaking branches and human footsteps circling my tent in the night. Just before five, I finished doing my triple checks on my lashings, the caretaker was nowhere to be seen so I rode up onto the main road and pulled the fence back into shape and turned west. I'd not gotten five miles down the road when it began to rain buckets. I couldn't wait to be in my barn, under shelter and out of this place.

I pushed on for another thirty minutes hoping it would pass but the drops just grew bigger, I began to sob in my helmet as the cold set in, I had tucked my trousers into my boots and the rain ran straight inside, filling up to my ankles, after about 170 miles I was losing the ability to shiver and decided I needed to dry up a little for the remaining 200. I pulled into a burger joint and stumbled after the dryer in the toilet. I spent nearly an hour barefoot in Tennessee piss, drying my boots and socks. A sweet full body girl from behind the register brought me a coffee and tissue, we spoke to each other softly. I wanted a kiss with my coffee. My mum, then my sister, then Sam, then Sophie and now Libby, wherever I turned there seemed to be a woman to look after me when I was lost. I saddled up and rode on, the big trucks spewed the standing water against my visor as I pushed through the grey.

    The directions I was given to Andy's farm were focused around two long dirt tracks and an American flag. I would ride along one track until I found the flag stuck in the ground, marking the turn to the second. I made the flag by early afternoon, the flag and me both stood there, on top of this Tennessee hill failing to fly in the wind under the weight of our drenched cloth, my wrinkled and whitened fingers turned the bars and twisted the throttle down the path, the road dug down the hill and cut into a crop of trees. I couldn't see the farm from the top of the track, beyond the trees were more trees, the fact was I'd never heard this man utter a single word, yet there I was riding down this path into a thick fog of green leaves, their branches drooped down under the weight of the falling water until they could hold no more, like a natural firework the leaf shot up flashing the water away. These blasts happened all around me throwing nature's breath deep into my skin. That was the only beauty I could find in the rain that day, the rest could go jump.

I hadn't stopped other than to feed Tina, and as I trundled down the track my front wheel sunk into the mud, flinging the bike left and right, the energy in my legs was not there to hold her properly, yet by some grace I got her fat rump down the slope, through the woods and onto a flat lay that opened to a large rolling field. The bike was a rodeo down that path, I knew I had smooth road tires on and a tonne of weight but I was scared with the honesty of my abilities that were now spewed across the pages for the days ahead. My soul had swung so low through the eleven hours of riding in the heavy cold rain and now I was losing all sense of confidence on a tiny track, and I hadn't got to Siberia yet, or Mongolia or Kazakhstan or Russia. I had no more tears to alleviate the heartbreak or shakes to warm my skin so I just hung my head and smiled.

Held up at the end of the track was a red-walled farmhouse with two metal barns, as I pulled down past the first barn the door began to roll and out hopped a work-dog picking a fight. Following soon after was Andy, a stocky man in work denim, a grey crew with a gruff beard hanging from his ears.

I rolled the bike through the barn doors and into the dry, this was the first time all day I had been without the skies falling on my shoulders. I kept moving the bike to where I had been marshalled, I took a shallow breath, it was all I could take, I had disintegrated under my jacket and needed my heart back.

'I was in two minds to turn tail and run.'

'Could you hear the banjo's playing?'

He was digging my humour and I his. The sadness of the day rolled away as I pulled my leg over the bike. We talked lightly as I started to roll my sleeping kit out next to where the dog was sleeping in the corner of the barn. I gravitated towards animals, I stood there looking over the dog's shoulder feeling protected.

Andy stopped me unpacking. His wife had made a bed in the house and I was to sleep there. I smiled and followed him in. The house was clean and homely, made entirely of wood, making it delightful to walk on barefoot. I showered and changed into dry clothes, my wet ones were taken by Andy's wife to be cleaned and dried.

'I hope you enjoy pizza, Paul.' Andy's wife hollered from the kitchen.

'I definitely do.' I shouted back

'I haven't had the chance to cook anything, I'm so sorry.'

'Don't you dare apologise, this is more than enough, I was happy to sleep with the dog in the barn.'

We sat and ate. I made a mess with the speed I consumed the food and they looked on in amazement. I looked up from the crumbs haloing my seat. 'I apologise; the pizza was too good.'

'Have you warmed up yet?'

I curled my toes over the wood.

'More than you'll ever know.'

They told me their story and the wholesome life they led here on their cattle farm. We spoke about the joys of cooking and family.

'People are too quick to get take out and ready-made meals.' I blurted, looking down at the pizza box, my face turned red. 'Then sometimes life gets in the way and then it really helps.'

They raised their eyebrows at me getting carried away and just carried on.

My face burnt with the happiness of their company, their sweetness for this drowned British rat that rolled through their door was just what I needed. As the night moved they spoke about the all-natural and organic beef they farmed. Andy hadn't run any further than the Rockies out west and had only been to the east coast once in all his fifty years, yet he had traipsed every inch of land from the delta to his doorstep, on dirt bikes and trucks and back again. He threw his stories of whirly birds, getting lost in the mountains at night and hosting dirt races on his farm.

By now his friend John from the local town was sharing the beers and narrating Andy's stories. A former US Ranger, John, who was broad, strong and kind-hearted produced a loud laugh that echoed through the house as he deconstructed my trip, only to conclude that doing this expedition with my experience and my bike was tantamount to suicide. I laughed nervously, putting the beer to my lips so I could hide my agreement. We folded into the night continuing our stories, belly laughs and beer. John had arranged for me to meet and stay with people for the next week or so as traversed the south, I couldn't be more grateful for to these people and the fun that was instore.

My bed sat in a large room, all wood panels and patchwork dolls, a huge safe standing taller than me on tip toes loomed in the corner, its dark blue paint merged into the shadows. I pulled the blanket high and was asleep quicker than I could remember.

The road out of town remained soft. The cumulus clouds had run east, leaving behind a mammoth blue sky leading all the way to Nashville and beyond. The road turned into a broad dry strip of asphalt running past the petite wooden houses of Crossville all the way to the horizon, the cold morning air rushed up under the chin of my helmet. Like cold water my eyes exploded open to the fresh weeping trees.

It was just under a tonne to Nashville so I arrived about 11am, riding up the hill on Broadway I rode past some washed up hippies clicking spoons and hands to a dusty song to get some money for food and weed. The sun was making up for yesterday's troubles with the heat running down the tip of my back and lungs. I kicked out the stand and leant her down, rolling my jacket over my luggage. I sat down beside the bike on the kerb to watch the cowboys and addicts walking by. It wasn't long until people wandered over, curious of the bike with foreign plates that sat in downtown Nashville. I told my story and posed for some photographs.

'Hey, are you from Canada?'

'No, no I am from England.'

'Fuck.'

'Well I've been living in Boston for the last few years and I'm now riding home.'

This would become the most common conversation I would have over the next three months of travelling, I never fully got used to this kind of attention. I tried to perfect my photograph face but I kept pulling this look as if I was trying to smile for a school photo whilst being given a vaccine in my butt cheek. A silver-haired cowboy loomed over to me, his air of pure craziness seemed to alleviate any awkwardness I was feeling. He rode up next to me with his silver boots and a tan hat, parking his electric bicycle, complete with two handlebars next to me and stood there and stared. I raised a hand and we shared our stories, he was a wandering kid from somewhere just not here, he proceeded to circle Tina for a full seven laps.

'You've got this all wrong,' he proclaimed
'Oh?'
'I can't believe you've made it this far.'
'It's all a work in progress, but any help you can give.'
'In '78 I cycled from Billings to Santa Fe.'

And off he went. The conversation fitting nicely into the craziness of the last few days.

I sat and drank a can of pop and watched the people wander the streets, I was craving to dive into the dark doorways and see the source of the music coming out, the place was screaming the blues, rock 'n' roll and country.

I needed a place to store my bike so I headed out of town to find a cheap motel, I found one that was under huge renovations so the room were super cheap. I dragged my bags and spare tires into a large room of Bakelite brown and creams. Out the window ran a junction box, signal towers and tracks holding grease covered locomotives. Two rough looking kids clambered on top of a cart and dropped inside, waiting for their ride to a better life.

I pulled on my old jeans and a t-shirt and walked the bridge back into town. I was sweating hard so I ducked into Tootsies. By the door was a tiny stage where a cowboy was singing a sad song with powerful lungs, I ordered a cold beer and rocked back and forth on my bar stool to the single drum beat. A dark-eyed barmaid told me her story across the graffiti strewn wood of the bar, not much of her story reached across the volume, her hands were deeply tattooed all the way up to her shoulders yet her stance swayed with an innocent ease, like a daffodil being held up by the wind. We spoke through movement as the sound of the country changed to doo-wop. A heavy couple sat down beside me wearing matching shirts. I stunk of the road and sweat. The woman wheeled around to show me her disgust, I bared my teeth at her and left.

My phone rang.

'Hey, Paul it's Jon, John's friend.'

'Hey man, where shall we meet?'

'A slight problem, my son is really not feeling well, I need to take him to the doctors'.

'There's no problem mate, just go. I'm fine, sort out your son.'

'Let me sort this I will call you back.'

I wandered off, it got me thinking of home and Libby and the vast spaces between us all. So I cut away from the maddening crowds and wandered down an uneven back street. I went through a black door at the bottom of some steps, a barman stood behind a tiny bar selling rye.

'A Makers please.'

'Sure thing, ice?'

'Please.'

I pushed the rim with my finger and looked at the bottom, my phone rang.

'Hey man it's Jon, my ex-wife is looking after the kid, let's meet up.'

Jon gave me directions to a bar. I made my way through the streets, arriving in time to see Jon waiting outside. We sat down at a three-tiered bar crammed with country fans and empty bottles. Jon worked in construction after a stint in the Navy. He was a gentle red haired kid, who had a natural way with women yet as we talked it was clear he had no way at all with the relationships that followed. We wandered the bars until he had to go collect his kid, he wanted another buddy of his to come meet me for dinner, so he drove me up the road to meet Dean, who arrived wearing dungarees over a tie-dyed shirt. He was huge like a bear and had a laugh to match. He sat down with all the waitresses greeting him like family, he ordered food for the pair of us as he sat with his arm around me laughing at his stories and mine. I howled with him, tears came down my cheeks from his endless jokes, I hadn't laughed like that in ages, maybe over a year, maybe even longer. Into the night we roared, imbued in the stranger's heart, Dean was like an uncle who I'd never met and we'd been kept apart by means outside of our control and now as we matched our lives together a warm love grew. He dropped me back by the bridge and I wandered home. I knew somehow I would see Dean again, maybe with Libby as well. Yeah, that would be cool.

When the sunset over Nashville a bit of me remained, tucked in the gutter, ready to drink open the blues and become a heretic among the cowboys and tourists.

I awoke early, hitting the road in a daze. I got a 100 miles down the road until I found myself stood in the morning air sipping on a coffee, hoping the caffeine would abate my headache brought on from the previous day's beer. Through the blur, a man a few inches taller than my six foot two, slowly approached, his upper girth only covered by a sleeveless leather jacket and faded tattoos. In typical American fashion he divulged his life story with little more than a half attempted smile. He proclaimed he was once a man in prison and a pilgrim of heroin, but now sober, he rode as the head of a motorcycle church for recovering addicts and bike enthusiasts. Before I knew what was happening we were holding hands, me, him, four of his congregation and his daughter, listening to this man scream and holler a prayer to the lord above, that my endeavours remained safe.

His daughter caught my eye and over her father's roar she whispered 'Take me with you', I fleetingly laughed and continued to listen to the prayer. It ended and there she stood still looking at me, I couldn't think of anything to say but 'There ain't no room on my bike?'. Her faced dropped further, as her eyes swelled with tears, she turned and walked away from me. A few miles down the road I thought of her pale wanting eyes, hoping she'd get free, her dad had found God, I hoped she found someone.

Tina and me rumbled away, vibrating all the way down past Memphis, down the banks and then for the first time in my life, I saw the river that was the Mississippi. Full of logs floating on the dirty melt water charging from Montana and the likes. I rode over her on a vast iron bridge, watching the water tumble away beneath my feet, I stopped there in the middle of the road just watching the present. There was no past or future to water.

I kicked onto Little Rock with the wind on my back. It felt like I was standing still, my old bike jacket and trousers turned out to be woefully underpowered for what had been thrown to me so far, so before I cut north to Conway I headed to a bike shop and invested in some heated gloves and a jacket liner. I pulled the bike apart and fitted the wires under the glorious Arkansas sunshine.

Flying past the slow cattle trucks all the way to sundown, I kissed the day goodnight around a campfire with today's family, five sweethearts who were friends again, of John. They gave me a bowl of food and a warm bed and most importantly their friendship. It was a sweet deal I was on, I would ride free all day and have a door open to me at the end.

The most difficult part of meeting with a new surrogate family was what I called the mass murder five, it was the first five minutes where we both hoped the other wasn't a killer. When else in the world would you let a twenty-something man with no fixed address stay in your house. When he has a motorcycle and a British accent.

The days we're blurring. I knew the day's number not the name of the day. I could have worked it out, but I was too busy and preoccupied with the side wind coming my way that had been there since leaving last night's family. It hounded and howled and whooped and screeched, it spiralled and pushed with no more dignity than a boot on an enemy's neck. All the way across Arkansas, through Russellville, Clarksville and Fort Smith, I leant the bike over to keep on the dead shot route I was taking into Oklahoma. The wind blew stronger, across Sallisaw, Henryetta and Shawnee. It threw giant balls of tumbleweed and dust across my path, endlessly smashing against my blackened spokes. I would pass a truck and the wind would abate, sending me into a wobble until the wind came back to punch my ribs, hip and shoulder. The beating continued all the way to Midwest city, past the corpses of armadillos, dogs and jacks littering the rain gutter. How I didn't end up like them, on my back with my legs in the air, while the flies ate was a mystery.

Tonight I was heading to Oklahoma City, I was staying with Rich, an old AMA racer and his wife, Ashley. Also friends of a friend, somehow connected to John from Tennessee. I pulled the bike into their garage, Tina sat amongst Italian superbikes and race prepped Suzuki's, workstations and a tornado shelter.

With the meet and greet over we headed into downtown Oklahoma, to watch a film called Fag Bug that was screening at the old Paramount studio. A true story about a girl who became a victim of a hate crime. She travelled the country telling her story and as she drove around the States, her girlfriend left and her popularity grew. A pretty little thing with too much time on the road, at the end of the film she rambled about her hardships and loneliness, no one had asked but yet there she was telling. I slumped in my chair as I fought my heavy eyes. We caught each other's gaze, she misjudged my bent hips for contempt and burnt my chest with her hazelnut eyes, I stuck out my tongue and screwed my nose, she smiled.

We went across the street to review the film over slices of pizza, behind us drunk cowboys, laughed out loud under the lights. I'd never been around cowboys before with their hats and boots but here they were filling the flat top buildings all the way to main street and back, I listened into the night to the greats Rich had met and raced against, but I couldn't hold concentration for the want of looking at the brims and spurless heels surrounding me.

Too much time had passed in the pizza place causing us to chase the gatekeeper down the street to get our car out of the parking lot. I laughed myself to sleep amongst the deep pillows and heavy blanket, what grandeur and oddity that had been my 29th birthday.

I was finding my place on this trip, it was falling together like centuries of evolution had been leading me to this point. I mean nothing beyond my own station but the path had been written and here I was. Why I set out on this trip was not something I could really pin to one single reason, maybe it was the logistical conundrum of the planning stage in all its beautiful chaos or the fear of the unknown, all sweet and out of reach. Or maybe I hoped the time alone would give me peace and time to learn of the world I cared so much about, but knew so little.

Looking down on a canopy of a forest makes us wonder what's below, wonder what it smells and tastes like, is it hot or cold, dry or humid, bright or dark. Tina could answer all those questions for me, but I was missing a trick, I was looking ahead, as always, not chewing the day as I should have been, laying back and enjoying this big wooden Oklahoma bed. My mind was already in gear for tomorrow, I stopped my mind and in an instant I felt very isolated, I stopped myself from crying and went to sleep.

I woke to a healthy breakfast of fruit and a bag of odds to keep me full on the road, all courtesy of my hosts. I watched Rich set up my suspension, it turned out that he'd made some beautiful race suspension for some top teams and noticed mine were all wrong. I sat in the saddle as we bobbed the bike up and down, changing all the dials getting it set for the miles ahead.

'It's the best you're going to get,' Rich answered

'Thank you and thank you, Ashley, for the everything.'

He confessed he'd missed work to help me out, I was so taken back I couldn't quite frame my words.

'Where are you heading for today?' Rich questioned

'Amarillo in Texas.'

'That's only 250 miles, you should go further, try for 500 at least.'

'That's too much for me, the way I ride, I stop for fuel and not much else, then I get time to wonder around my destination.'

'But you could see so much more, in Alaska I covered 10,000 miles in three weeks.'

I thanked Rich & Ashley for the amazing hospitality and rode on to Texas, all the way to Amarillo. I felt self-conscious because of Rich's comments, it made me feel lazy and slow. Once I had calmed down I saw the facts, he was on the road only for a few weeks and I would be out here for months. This was my trip not his and it had to be done my way else what was the point? It was hard choosing not to listen to someone with real experience and go your own way, maybe he was right and I was wrong, but I had to find out the hard way.

My surrogate families had looked after me, made me laugh and had become part of this story, yet tonight I wanted my own space to throw my stuff out across a room, eat early then pass out. So I decided to book into a motel, the place was full of truckers and was a stumble from some tasty looking steak restaurants. One had a ginormous statue of a cowboy, who was waving his hat to the hot blue Texas sky, his yellow shirt must have been as big as a house. I stood next to his boots looking up. This had to be the place to eat.

I went through a set of paddle doors and sat at an old 70s Cadillac which was also the bar. A pale kid from Massachusetts, living down here working on the pumps earning money to take home told me of the motorbikes he owned and how sorely he missed his family. The waitress passed me a large padded menu, I chose a 27oz steak, their smallest, the waitress curled her lips when I ordered, screaming across the order to the kitchen "one cowgirl steak medium rare for the gentleman at the bar." I blushed and tried to sink into my bar stool as smiles from around the bar burnt. I sunk a few beers as the buttery steak disappeared. I kept my head low as I left the bar enjoying the world that was preoccupied in everything but me. I laid sprawled naked on the sheets laughing, god damn this adventure stuff is fun! I fell asleep at 7p.m. and slept like that in the heat of the night all the way through to daybreak.

    I had placed in all the petrol stations along my route on my GPS. I had about 110-mile range give or take depending on the wind direction, elevation gains, heat and traffic. All of these factors on the bike cause me to be careful how far I wondered off the beaten path. I was barrelling down the road towards Santa Fe, New Mexico. I was pushing 107 miles on the trip and was already on my reserve, but I knew that around the bend was a station and hopefully somewhere I could get a bite to eat. I was getting hungry today, even though I'd eaten everything the motel buffet had to offer.

    The sign of the petrol station rose high into the sky, their neon logo slowing turning on top of a large seventy-foot pole. So many petrol stations used these to mark their location, signalling to the weary traveller that a safe haven was ahead. As I rolled closer my heart began to sink, the place was derelict, out of business. Although the sign was still spinning, the buildings were boarded and empty, apparently for some time. In an instant panic, I tapped the screen of my GPS and calculated the next petrol station was over sixty-five miles ahead or seventy-seven miles behind me. I calculated that my best bet was to continue on as far as I could, I didn't have any off-route stations programmed therefore I couldn't afford to explore and end up in the back and beyond without fuel and no passer-by, so off I trundled down the main corridor.

Too increase my aerodynamic efficient I laid flat on the tank and slowed to fifty, I came around a corner to find a strong wind on my back. There it stayed as I rolled on down the hill for nearly sixty miles, the bike just kept on running, somehow the world was smiling on me, the gods of the ancient world resurrected themselves and push me and Tina. As people watched me roll into the petrol station they were totally unaware of the hope that I was holding onto in that helmet. I stood next to my bike going through the convoluted routine of accessing my fuel cap when a woman screamed across the courtyard in a strong and brash Texan accent.

'And what do you think you're doing?'

'I'm riding around the world.'

'On a scooter?'

'It's actually a 900.'

She gave me a look like I had grossly wronged her by questioning her definition of Tina

'A scooter compared to American bikes,' she snapped as she turned away.

Someone was having a bad morning. I had been looked after by the gods and there she was having burger withdrawals. I smiled and kept the retorts to myself, fuelled up and left.

The day fell away in a daze uneventfully as I rolled up Glenn's driveway on the outskirts of Santa Fe, the last of John's friends. We went down to Santa Fe for dinner and drank some beers over enchiladas and tacos. We continued drinking at an ice hockey game Glenn's buddies were playing in. In a mixture of tiredness and repetition the evening passed by without much registering and soon I found myself asleep amongst the move in boxes still occupying his spare room.

Glenn went to work early and left me to lock up. I said goodbye to the dogs and rode northwest towards the four corners, a place where Utah, Colorado, New Mexico and Arizona met. I wandered the dusty lot, amongst the Native American stalls selling stone-tipped arrows and hand woven badges. The shacks encompassed a brass disc set into the earth marking the four states colliding. I ran around the plate as fast as I could to cover all four states, I did a dance in my boots in the centre and laughed like a dog barking at the moon.

An old couple approached to take a photo.

'Where you heading?'

'Home,' I replied with a smile.

'Where'd you start?'

'Boston, what about yourselves?

'Oh we just drove over from Wyoming; we're heading down to the Grand Canyon.'

'Amazing, my girlfriend is from Wyoming.'

'Oh really, whereabouts?'

'Spring Rocks, something like that.'

'Do you mean Rock Springs? We're fifteen miles down the road from there.'

'No way, amazing her dad is the doctor there.'

'He's married to Karen.'

'Exactly.'

We agreed the world was small between the photo smiles.

They pulled out and rolled south as I continued west towards Kanab in Utah. This would be my turning point for the Rockies and the north towards Canada. I could easily imagine the hardships of the frontiersmen and women that rode horse and cart in these lands with no idea what lay beyond the Rockies. The deserts rolled further than the horizon could imagine, the only evidence of man in this dust lid was the pipes running to and from the refineries and oil drills. The sun baked me into my seat and danced off the chrome of the exhaust. The road had been laid so smooth that I could just lay back on my bags, rest my clutch hand on my thigh and ride, I sat in fifth at sixty miles per hour as the world spun beneath me. The flat open deserts started to flash with orange stone and sand, the soft stone continued all around until life could no longer hold itself back as lush green bushes and trees sprouted from the walls of the orange cliffs and mountains. It was an assault on the senses as they grew more vigorously and dense as the miles drew on.

I had not a single problem with Tina, the weight was no longer there, the fresh new tires were scuffed in and the suspension was a cloud. Petrol stations now readily appeared and the miles flew by. I decided to treat myself to a break along with an apple so I jumped the bike down an embankment and pulled under the shade of a hardy tree. The terra-cotta sand was soft so I used a rock to steady the side stand, I hunkered down next to the bike under the shade of the tree as my back grew warm from the engine cover. I crossed my ankles out onto the ground, feeling my joints crack and strain with their new found freedom. The stillness felt good. I inspected my skin looking at the lines the sun had drew and the dirt that had built up. My wrists were especially dark, with a thick band of fine dirt, that had grown between my glove and jacket. I slowly fingered the dirt into a pile and blew it to the sky. I was restless and riding the miles seemed to do little. I wanted to get drunk, fuck the cost. Kanab was magical, all I needed was stirrups and Tina to morph into a horse and I would have been a real cowboy wandering into this town.

    I arrived at the motel and pulled Tina behind a small wall, hiding her from the road. I walked across the motel carpark past a big blue '65 Deville as an old man with a face like a cake that had been left out in the rain grinned at me as his wife painted her nails in the doorway and complained to everyone in earshot about the food. I disappeared into the dark of my room as I stowed away my kit. I decided on a thick flannel shirt and jeans as the shower had run ice cold. Locking the door behind me, I said goodbye to the couple still arguing outside and walked off down main street.

    I started to sweat heavily under the dense cotton shirt causing me to stop every few steps to cool, as I stared in a window full of old cameras, a reflection of saloon doors swinging in the wind behind me caught my eye. In the shadows I couldn't believe what I saw... between the hum of wiry hikers and travelling hippies shuffled waiters carrying six shooter pistols on their hips. I turned and watched. Why did people hold on to the past? Was it a personal view or were things actually better? I can't think that having guns on the hips of waiters is a sign of good times, other than the effect on the tip jar.

    I fell into a box diner with blue walls and nylon seats, quickly slipping into a bottle of red wine. I hoped I could alleviate the heat coming for the forty eyes sat in the corner of their sockets hoping to answer the question, why was he sat alone? Maybe they were right and I needed someone to ride with, fix the bike with and just have a good laugh. I fell into a pool of self-consciousness. I tried to start a conversation but my mouth decided to mumble and my eyes rolled down over my cheeks. I drank more and ate dessert, a rich chocolate cake that stuck to my teeth. The alcohol brought me to giggle and huff at the table bringing to an end to my dinner and reason to hightail out of there. My mind was racing frantically at past and future transgressions so as I stumbled into the cool night air, I calmed and let my temperature abate. I had really achieved my goal of getting drunk, as I fell from pillar to post laughing to myself all the way home.

    I awoke to a full stomach from the last night's feed, the dense force was comforting. Maybe home and my place in this world lay within chocolate cake. I yawned my way out to the parking, it was before seven and the sun hard barely broke the mountain ridge. I stood next to Tina just breathing the fresh air when I realized a good three pints of oil sat below my motorbike, reflecting the undercarriage in the morning light. I removed the smash guard and cleaned her belly. I sat on the frigid floor waiting for a definitive sign on where the leak originated. Tina was now a proper Triumph. An accolade I wasn't keen on receiving. I sat there and waited and waited then drip, tiny molecules painted my shin, it was the neutral switch indicator. A tiny plug that went into the engine housing, it made a green light glow on my handlebars when I was in neutral. The light worked and neutral was easily found. A calmness sat in me, the next workshop I could get parts from was two days' ride. I marked the level of oil on the small window that sat on the side of the crankcase and rode out.

The calmness from the mornings discovery remained with me as I climbed my way through Bryce Canyon national park. Closely grouped trunks of rock grew from the ground and appeared to have been turned brown and orange by the big sky overhead. The road came to ahead and stopped at a vista screaming out as far as I could see. The cacophony of orchestral colours danced in the morning light, the yellows chimed and the blues fluted. The power of nature's beauty glistened within in its fragility, as I took my place alongside and felt connected to the harmony. The shadows echoed the booms of the greys and the wind trumpeted the reds of the dirt. I climbed over the railings and sat down on a ledge that begged me to slide down its smooth face and into the abyss below. What was in last nights red wine?

A few hundred feet below me a natural bridge had been formed by the slow erosion of weather, leaving swirled walls and beautiful archways. I felt constricted by the bike, I wanted to walk down into the canyons but I couldn't leave the bike with all the kit on it. I looked for a hiding spot but without any luck.

I saddled up and rode back down the trail to the head and cut north. I couldn't believe I was heading north, so much of the United States was behind me and I was heading towards the Canadian border. I became overwhelmed and had to stop the bike. I breathed deeply until my stomach could expand no more and repeated that until my heart rate reduced. I felt so alone and happy, so wildly optimistic of what lay ahead, everything was so beautiful and new, the air running around my neck whispered its wisdom as I rode on to Salt Lake City.

I had been listening to the *Exile on Main Street* album on my phone as it echoed my mood perfectly, singling loudly as I rode laying back on my bags. Slowly a smell started to form and unlike others that had come my way, this one was staying with me. It was the unmistakable smell of burning plastic. I had developed a system that my phone would sit in my map case that was attached to the top of my tank back, alongside that was my watch and the day's paper map. This worked perfectly, I could see all the information I needed at a glance, listen to my music and keep the weight down in my pockets. It was perfect until my system thoroughly unravelled itself. I had no clue about the mutiny that had occurred or when because I was still blissfully listening to my music. When I looked down to check the time I found a completely empty map case, no phone, no map and no watch. I pulled over to the side of the road, skidding to a halt. Confused, as I was still listening to the music, I looked down the right side of my bike to find the source of if the smell and see my phone hanging on the end of my headphones, happily melting into my exhaust. I recovered my phone but my maps and watch were lost, the first casualties of the trip. I hoped a racoon or an armadillo is now sporting a bright orange dive watch and is able to give directions to lost travellers.

 I secured my phone back in the map case and let the remaining plastic burn off as I filled up at an automated petrol station. An amazing concept, you come in, you fill up, you pay and you get out, all the work, all the pay. If we as a society, work towards complete efficiency what are we left with? Idiosyncrasies are the cuts in the fabric of life that expose its beauty.

 The day passed with no other incident and the oil level in the engine remained high as the corporate towers of Salt Lake City started to rise from the dirt. With its five-lane veins pumping people into the chaos, it was a welcome sight. The energy and frivolity that only a city can hold is something I grew to love when I lived in London. I was craving the mix, creativity and variety that are held between the mass-produced windows and dirty walls. This city also held my girlfriend's sister Jo, and her fiancé, James. Although I hadn't met them in person I felt a certain connection born from a lonely road and a common love. Just south of Salt Lake City lay a bike shop that held the parts I needed to stop the oil leak, they needed the bike for two days giving me a time to get to know Jo and James.

We spent the next two days drinking in the bars and laughing over home cooked dinner and had decided to drive out to the mountains to celebrate the final day of the ski season. As we rode up the mountain pass to the resort, I marvelled in the alien sensation of riding in a car, the world passed so quickly, around bends at great speed all without a single breath of air pushing against my body. I was so used to taking corners at a certain speed, so much so I felt myself bracing as we weaved the snake backed mountain roads to the base of the mountains.

I checked in with the bike shop as they said the part would be in by lunchtime, the phone barely rang as I stood and listened to a monotone man waffle on about the hardships of his day and that he hadn't understood the urgency for the part and it would be sometime the following week. My heart sunk, four more days put a huge amount of pressure on the schedule because of the deadline for shipping my bike to Korea and I wanted to enjoy the roads of the Pacific northwest. Having half of a week removed from my schedule at this point was hard to swallow. I knew that once I was off the boat and onto Russian soil I could afford more time, but now was hard to absorb. I explained this all to the sales clerk yet his tone maintained itself in an unimpressive state. I told myself things could have been worse and that I could keep my budget in check by staying on the couch at Jo's. I worked out a more direct route to Seattle to get back the distance lost from the week and had myself back on schedule.

With the extra time to kill I thought it prudent to explore Salt Lake City, which is the home of the Latter Day Saints or Mormons, so we decided to spend the following day wandering their grand churches and museums. Jo and I wandered ahead as James put money in the meter, we stopped and waited for James next to some flowers growing around the base of a tree.

'It's amazing isn't it!' Jo marvelled.

'What is?' I enquired.

'Whenever there is some snow the flowers blossom after the melt.'

'I know right. It's as if the snow was made of water or something.'

I placed a large grin on my face as she rolled her eyes at my sarcasm, it was a good litmus for me to understand my comfort levels, the more sarcastic I became the more at home I was. I was forgetting the troubles of the delays, oil leaks and the enormity of the miles ahead. Towards the end of my fifth day in Salt Lake, after spending time on the couch watching day time TV I was looking forward to the road, to be just heading on. I picked Tina up thanked Jo and James and rode west.

My next stop was Wendover, the home of the Bonneville Salt Flats International Speedway. It was early morning and the sky was a cold clear blue, a single smooth road led me to the famous sign of Bonneville, what's great racers had run their tires over the exact same ground I now stood on. The Bonneville sign was a centimetre-thick piece of black metal, with a variety of emblems, cars, bikes and rocket ships etched into its surface. The smooth metal was riddled with bullet holes created by bored kids.

Being April the salt was still heavily logged with water, the low-lying sun turned the flats into silver as far as the eyes could see. A polished canvas with a watercolour painting of the sky, if only I could frame this moment. I closed my eyes like a camera shutter and told myself to imprint this in my memory for eternity, never to be erased or forgotten. I stepped down from the road down onto the salt, as I wanted to recreate the famous photo of Rollie Free breaking the speed record back in the 1940s. As my weight shifted onto my front foot, it sank into the salt leaving a pocket that was quickly filled by water. I tested other places sinking even further, the limitations of leaving so early in the year for this trip was becoming apparent. Yet I couldn't come all this way and not have a picture of Tina on the salt flats, but as I rode onto the salt the front slipped sideways and rear spun, I used all of my strength to stop the bike from going down and retreated back onto the tarmac. I felt the teeth of my off-road tyres that were strapped to my luggage and hoped they would help on the thousands of kilometres in Siberia, Mongolia, Russia and Kazakhstan.

I took in the view for as long as the camera roll in my head would allow then got back on the bike. The swing of my leg between my tank bag and my rear rack was becoming so common I wouldn't even register how I got in the seat from standing, the feeling of the seat between my legs felt like home and the push of my helmet on my jaw made me feel connected. I just wanted to ride. It was becoming both my cause and effect to be on the road, the bike meant I could be out exploring and the road gave my bike and me a home.

As I pulled into the town of Wendover, I soon realised it was a letdown to say the least. The steroid American muscle cars were non-existent and the 1950s hourglass girls were definitely not diving into the swimming pools occupying the front of many of the motels. The only things hanging lose were the welcome signs above the motel receptions. Wendover seemed nothing more than a girl who had been kissed once and been left wanting.

On one side of the mile, sat the dilapidated motels interlaced with signs for the pending state border where gambling was legal. The other side of the road sat deserted diners and breakers yards full of rusted steel and old tires. The eerie town made me want to stay close to my bike. This was not a place to be right now, I needed people, even if I didn't speak with them.

I rode the up the street with my helmet off and pulled into a sandwich shop, I walked inside and ordered a burger and a shake. I sat next to the window looking at my bike enjoying the burger, bacon and cheese.

I sat there thinking on what lay ahead, I had twelve more countries to cross before I could stand still, sleep in a bed I knew and have the touch of someone I loved. Crossing into Canada wasn't going to be easy, I was fortunate enough to be issued a second passport by the British Embassy allowing me to avoid any unwanted attention associated to my American visa whilst I was in Russia, Mongolia and Kazakhstan. The only issue, I needed to enter Canada on my new passport to allow me to board my flight to Korea. So I needed everything to be in order. But how can you leave a country on a passport that has no record of you ever entering? My plan was to exit on my old passport and use my new one to enter Canada. I was scared they would question me and I would be exposed for having two passports. All I needed was either of them to be confiscated and the trip would be seriously delayed if not over. I pushed my eyelids firmly into the sockets allowing maximum light to enter into my retinas, I was focused and ready for the border challenges. The border would not stop me. If at first, I don't succeed, just smile harder. I'll charm my way through, hopefully!

I bought some cans of pop and sweets and took them to my hotel room. I got naked and walked the room to enjoy the freedom. A film played on my computer as I ate the chocolate to my heart's content. I was breaking down what I had achieved, I was subconsciously supporting myself, you've done over two-thirds of the States already, you're on the last stretch, your first country is almost complete. You haven't crashed yet, the weather has only been bad for 7% of the days so far, what an amazing number considering the time of the year.

The following morning, I hit the road with purpose. I was on the road to Boise with the determination to meet people. I had spent the previous thirty-six hours alone and I needed that time, to figure out the mental hurdles and let myself off. Just like riding a motorcycle the success of the trip was a balancing act, a balance between my own thoughts and time with others. I set out to understand the world around me. The expanses I rode were vast, maybe in context to what lay ahead it was nothing more than heavily inhabited turf, gilded with smooth tarmac. In context to the trip so far it was open space that would allow your lungs to expand out through your ribs to the horizon. Life fell into place; I'd become part of the cycle. A beautifully intricate system, of giving and taking, where nature was the master and yielded for no one. Heaven has to be a place on this rock, under this sky, because then and only then will we treasure what we have now.

I had booked myself into the only hostel in town, it was cheap and right in the centre of Boise. The 303 miles to its doorstep passed by uneventfully until I struggled to find a parking spot, there were specific bike bays but the bikers I asked about the security and the ability to park overnight responded with shrugs and silence. I found a covered car park. By loading my shoulders and hands I was able to take all my kit from my bike in one go. I crashed through the hostel doors in my riding suit holding tyres, bags, a helmet and gloves. My riding gear was great at protecting me whilst I sat there enjoying the open road yet any physical exertion soon had me cherry faced and pouring in sweat.

A podgy necked man with an unshaven face came from the office which seemed to double as a bedroom and welcomed me into the hostel as his hands showed his confusion of the items I was carrying. I briefly explained my trip as he showed a corner of his bedroom I could safely store my gear. I walked across the hall and sat down on the lower bunk. I was here to make a friend or two and hopefully have a laugh, the only laughs I'd been having since arriving here were my own created by my near misses or moments of hysteria on what the hell was I doing riding a motorcycle around the world.

Two guys, that must have been in their mid-thirties sat playing a video game and didn't notice me as I sat down on the green corduroy couch beside them. I watched them play for a while and studied the room. The building was utilitarian with the pipes running across the walls and ceilings. They had tried to decorate the place with murals and posters, but they had faded and clung to the dirt that seemed so abundant in the windowless room. Their game ended and they turned my way with a smile.

'I'm Paul.'

'I'm Derek.'

We shook hands, Ryan was too far away, so I just raised a hand.

I dug into their backgrounds and found they were both from Boise, lost souls that had not strayed far. We continued to talk and their answers brought a sadness to the room. I changed tact.

'So what's fun to do around here?' I said looking at the door.

'There is a wall out back full great of art and graffiti, let's wait for Sarah and we can all go,' Derek answered

I didn't know whether I should feel sad or proud of Ryan and Derek. They were so far off course from a normal life, which in so many ways were noble and grand but they had not gotten far on their dreams and now lived with a pseudo family in a dank hostel. I was half way between a hippy in a tent and one day being the boss of my own global company. I related heavily to their wandering spirit but saw the sadness their eyes could never hide. I knew that now this expedition had begun nothing was going to stop me, other than serious injury or death. I wouldn't confess this determination willingly but I knew deep down very little was going to hold me back. I felt an internal apprehension, a fear and disappointment deep down like I was acknowledging their lives as my own, maybe it stemmed from my upbringing and the wanting to get away. I would be lying if I said I didn't crave success, I looked up to people like Ranulph Fiennes and Richard Branson. As I continued to talk with Ryan and Derek I wanted to click my fingers to their beat of life, if the world exploded now, I would be the fool as I constantly time travelled in my mind onto future tasks and back to past events, they seemed so content with the now, in an 'I have nothing left but now' kind of way, yet my drive kept them at arm's length. Sarah soon arrived, she seemed flustered but happy to be around Derek. She must have been a good fifteen years younger than him causing me to feel a slight sense of anger that his half-assed attempt at life might affect her. 'Run you fool' I bellowed in my head.

 We walked out into the street and crossed the road, a gravelled back alley led us to a long stretch of bricks that were covered in a vast array of art from businessmen jumping to their death with a blissful look on their faces, monkeys getting high and Hendrix turning into a flower. They didn't know who had done any of the work but came here regular to see if anything had changed, I told them of a similar place in London, under a train station where the like of Banksy got their name, but my story seemed missed.

I wandered back to the hostel, my expectations for frivolity were long dead. I laid down on my bed to let the tiredness of the day's ride set in. I forced my fingers between the slats of the mattress on the bunk above me to stretch out my arms. I rose and fell with the weight of sleep and needed to revive myself. I stood under the shower as the hot water washed new life into my body, I changed and headed back to the lounge. A new kid called Sam stood leant against the kitchen counter playing with a knot in his woollen sweater. Derek and Steve were back at the TV playing games, the sun had all but gone leaving behind nothing but the need to get drunk. Sam had given up on sorting out his knot and decided to tag along, the bars copied each other with neon signs for the beer they sold and smokers huddled like penguins outside, hiding the cigarettes as if they were reading porn in the presence of a priest.

We found two seats at the end of a wooden bar, two burgers came upon a mountain of fries and were soon lost under falls of beer. Sam was in town for a conference about ecology and was on a tiny budget, a bright kid with a wicked laugh that was keen to tell his stories and I was content to listen. I got dinner yet we skipped on paying for the beers as they had drained too quickly into our guts and now we lacked the coin to cover the charge. We made a run for it, laughing loudly as we turned the corner proud of our small rebellion.

We found another bar and moved onto whisky, the glasses again soon stacked up but this time, we felt obliged to pay if only to avoid a lynching. We walked in contented silence back to the hostel and passed out.

I awoke with a blinding hangover. This was the first time I had let my guard down on this trip, three weeks had almost passed since leaving Boston and I was finally willing to ease up on myself. I had appointed a British Military Drill Sergeant in my head to keep me moving, avoid unnecessary risk and ultimately remove the heart of the expedition.

I was finally learning the cost of heading out alone. Whilst I was able to create my own schedule and agree on whims in direction, the foods I carried and the places I could stay. I had no one with whom to share ideas, fears and look at one another for encouragement. I had walked a path of my own since leaving primary school. I was used to doing things alone and I prided myself with independence and self-reliance, it had got me to London, it had got me to Boston, it had me on the back of this bike. I knew that if I had waited for a friend to accompany me on most of my endeavours I'd still be waiting in my hometown looking sorry for myself.

That said, whenever I did find a friend that was willing to accompany me on an adventure, once we were back down on the valley floor, drinking a beer to congratulate ourselves on our accomplishments my mind raced with the next task and the buddy would wave me goodbye and I would be onto the next, which nine times out of ten would be the complete opposite to the last feat. I'd finished climbing Mont Blanc so I decided to start a magazine, I interviewed Noam Chomsky and a satirical cartoonist from the Guardian, proposed ideas on fossil fuel consumption and started a charity for depressed young professionals. I made four editions and ran out of money. I then started a fitness company training people in a park in London, it was fun to be outdoors but I wasn't challenged mentally. But now, right here, I was fucked. I was alone and scared, I had gone beyond anything I had known and a thought Nazi had taken over in my head keeping me focused on the end of the day, the next 330 miles, which was an ideal distance to travel during the day as I could get 110 miles per tank and two stops seemed enough rest.

Whether it was the hangover or something else, I didn't want to get caught in this mental rut so I flung my leg onto my bike and looked down to the tank bag, the handle bars and speedometer, my arms moved themselves to the grips and I was home. The circumference felt right. I rode mostly with a pair of cut wrist leather gloves, the kind cowboys wore. They used to be the colour of sand and now the oil and dirt and burns made them dark and soft and black. Looking at them made me feel at home.

I reflected on my surrogate families, all that I could remember, the wooden floors of the farmhouse in Crossville, the cardboard boxes next to me on the floor in Albuquerque, the prayer circle in Virginia and the bullet holes in the Salt Flat. Damn, what a life. I was truly blessed by the hearts of so many, I had been waiting for this my whole life, a true adventure. I must move towards home, around the world.

My next stop was the Pacific Ocean; the last Saltwater I would see until the English Channel well over 15,000 miles later.

SEATTLE

I completed my ride from Boise to the Pacific Ocean, easing into Seattle. I was wet from the mountains that had pushed me up into the clouds a few miles before the city border. I walked down to the shore and stood there, beyond the bay brawled the Olympic mountain range, proud and covered in snow. I hopped up and down on the spot with excitement, I had covered this huge country, all on my Triumph. I spun down the street knowing who I was. The air was wet and cold, sending me back to my childhood holidays camping in Dorset and Devon, the sea spray on my skin made me feel fresh.

I found a bar running into the last happy hour. I pushed my teeth through a dish of cold salmon, sinking four beers. I left the bar and turned the corner, it was time for a harder drink. I walked the steps to a speakeasy and squeezed myself down to a glass of gin, a couple to my right ran the small talk with the effortlessness ease that only an American accent can bring. They compared the collection of spirits to other places they had been and talked about the crookedness of the stairs that led to the bar, they played the jokes and the conversation just kept on flowing. I continued to get buzzed amongst the river of their words and the cheap gin that poured into my glass. I sat there until I had finished nearly half the bottle, my cheeks flew red and I smiled to the bartender and left. Night had come over the city and I walked the streets as the world spun around me in happiness, the gin sunk further into my abilities and I walked around the streets knocking into people and places.

I checked into the dated multi-story hotel in downtown, imagining days gone of seedy men pushing women and drugs from the corners and dark alleyways. Life was regained in my weary bones after a hot shower and I glided down over the clean sheets and soon fell asleep.

The following day I was to head north, I was staying with a couple that was following my trip online and been kind enough to extend me an offer of a bed and a meal. I weaved my way through tall trees and beautiful homes and ended in a cul-de-sac with Mike and Morgan waiting in their driveway for my arrival. They welcomed me in and we chatted away with ease. I was envious of their set up, their beautiful home amongst the tall trees, shouldered in green. If a child were to draw a tree this what they would look like, strong brown trunks erupting from the dirt, dressed in beautiful green needles. What a beautiful piece of design, where something can exist so high into the skyline yet only stand there to enhance the sky.

I got changed and headed next door to accompany Mike and Morgan at a neighbour's birthday party and BBQ. Just like every other family up to this point I was quizzed and welcomed in. I stood barefoot in the kitchen sipping a beer curling my feet into the heated tiles. The father of the house stood next to the BBQ, as he turned the meat and glazed the skin. He stood tall and broad as if one of the trees gave him to the world, he was a natural family guy with a long laugh. We ate and sang happy birthday late into the evening, as I listened to plans for an upcoming wedding I thought of tomorrow. It was a milestone and a potential nightmare, I had two passports, one with an expired visa and the other with no reference to me ever entering the United States.

Morning came around and I drank coffee with Mike and Morgan in their kitchen. Mike had outlined a route for me to the border involving a short ferry ride out to set islands nestled in the sound.

As I waited in line for the ferry a Harley pulled up next to me, a short round man got off and stood next to me in full leathers. He removed his helmet and tucked his gloves away, we stood there sweating in our full suits in the midday sun. We talked. He'd had the engine rebuilt twice, and clocked over 100,000 miles on his Harley, all in the States. We rode our bikes to the bow of the ferry, where we were stopped by a thin chain that served as our only protection between the water and us. A small sign was bolted to the wall showing the different whales that lived in the area.

As the ferry pulled away we started our conversation back up, I listened to the stories of the land he knew, the big open spaces and intricate islands of northwest America. His home was wherever the great sky touched North America and as I listened he seemed to know every inch back and forth, the roads he had not rolled down were few and far between. Harley Davidson's were common in America, chrome oozed from every surface yet here was a Harley that has been turned matte by the sun, humble, honest and a genuine badass.

I suddenly knew that even when I got home I would have many more miles to go. I was born to wander, I wasn't seeking to tick a box, it was the moving I loved. He told me about the years that he had rolled over the roads in order to clock up those miles. He had missed seasons for money and family reasons but he always looked ahead, knowing the next corner held a chance to turn the ignition key.

I watched him with a gentle awe as he inspected my kit, his brow would bunch and relax as if to acknowledged my error and leave it for me to discover. His curiosity would not allow him to keep quiet on why I was carrying spare tires, it was a mistake I had made months earlier. It was a late night kit list review going over every last detail and within the blinkers of what I needed, into the basket went a pair of Continental TKCs. I couldn't afford to leave them and trying to sell them was hard due to the obscure size. One benefit that had come out of it was they acted as a pseudo backrest, on the broad straight roads of New Mexico and Texas I could ride resting on the tires with only a few fingers on the throttle. He said I should have shipped them to Vancouver where I was to depart for Korea. He was so obviously right, I looked at my feet.

The ferry pulled into Whidbey Island. Just before we were about to roll away Jim dug his hand into his pocket and passed me the contents, it was a little over $20.

'It's all I have on me,' he professed.

I thanked him and we parted our separate ways. The sun was on my side and the warmth of the day was beginning to rise. I agreed to myself to pass forward the kindness of Jim. The roads were beautifully quiet and smooth, navigation was simple as there was only one road, so I relaxed in the groove and rolled my bike into the turns. Mike had told me about Deception Pass a beautiful and must see gorge a few miles into the island chain, it was discovered by George Vancouver when he believed Whidbey Island was a peninsula, only after Vancouver sent Joseph Whidbey in a small boat to investigate further, resulting in a circumnavigation, Vancouver declared the land an Island, and promptly named it Whidbey. At the head of Whidbey Island sat the gorge. Close to 200ft deep ending in heavy churning turquoise water caused by the full strength of the Pacific being squashed into a 300-foot gap. The sheer power was terrifying even from the bridge railing above. Letting the sun warm my back I sat with the trees and wind for a while eating an apple preparing myself for the Canadian border.

Further complicating my issues was that Korea also required proof of onward travel and this moment all I had was poor photocopy of the ferry boarding pass. For now, I had to exit a country on a passport that had no record of me ever arriving. I had finished my tour of the islands before the border and now I was back on the mainland. Soon came the sign for Canada and I simply couldn't hold it in, so I screamed and howled. I rose up on my pegs and yanked the throttle open, I soon realised I was doing nearly ninety stood up in a controlled military area near border control.

I slowed, sat back on the seat and started to laugh. I filtered through the traffic and before I knew it I was at passport control. I had barely got my helmet off when the American exit cleared me to proceed into Canada. The speed in processing me caught me off guard. I paused looking straight at the border guard, waiting for the questions, my charm was ready, poised on my tongue. Silence fell, I smiled and hurried to put my helmet back on, but decided it was quicker to hoop it over my mirror, lurching forward I headed into Canada. I pulled over a mile or so up the road to recompose and get my helmet back on. I rechecked my passport, all in order, fuck yeah! Stress over nothing!

VANCOUVER

I arrived in Vancouver with fresh baked cookies that Morgan had made for me that morning. I stopped somewhere in the city centre, I had given myself a little over five days in Vancouver, to allow time to sort out the shipping of Tina to Korea and catch up with a close friend who lived and worked in Vancouver.

I started to think of a life that lay ahead, beyond this trip and beyond this year. Mike and Morgan had a great way of life, surrounded by thoughtful and funny neighbours in mountains and water, city life nearby and woodland peace in the back yard, and most importantly each other. The thought of a life spent with another fought in my mind like children on a seesaw, desperate to feel the ground beneath their feet. I longed to hold Libby's hand and feel her touch. Could I spend my life with her or would I just become another penultimate boyfriend before she married another, just as I had been in every other relationship?

I walked away from those thoughts for a few hours and forced myself to be present. Vancouver is constantly ranked as one of the best places in the world to live as it strikes a beautiful balance between outdoor pursuits and the plethora of creativity only a big city can contain. I had never been, yet an old housemate, Johnny, was here, now working for Harbor Air as a seaplane pilot. His outlook was similar to mine so I was excited to explore his finds of the city and hopefully spend a day or two in the nearby Coast Mountain range.

I rolled up to Jonny's house. It sat on a long leafy road amongst a calm suburb of Vancouver. Johnny was working for a few more hours and I had no aspirations other than to watch the world go by. I sat down on the kerb next to the bike and foraged my panniers for food. A crushed packet of ready salted crisps came to hand and as I prized the packet open I wrapped my shoulder blades around a young tree freshly planted at the bottom of his drive.

I had done it, I had made my way across North America and felt a pride quite different to any other project I had completed. It was denser and more silent. I didn't want to say a word about it, just keep it selfishly to myself.

I finished the crisps and folded the packet into a triangle, flicking it into my open pannier. Looking down at the bug graveyard on my trousers I noticed that the burn hole made by my exhaust on the outer shell had grown bigger, I fingered the whole only to make it bigger still. I decided to repair the hole with a lattice of gaffer tape, whilst I marvelled at my handy work Johnny came home and we hauled my luggage inside. He explained about the burrow-browed landlord that resided in the apartment next door and his strict policy against people staying. We devised a plan on getting in and out that was more elaborate than some of the Berlin wall escapades, but during my week stay, I was proudly able to come and go without detection.

Johnny was running a double shift and said I could get on a flight with him that afternoon. He headed back down to the seaport as I tucked my luggage into a corner of the room. I rolled out my trusty pair of jeans and a somewhat clean t-shirt, albeit an oil stain from someplace or other, I pulled the hem away from me so I could examine the stain closer. I felt proud and chose to wear it like a medal. I rode down the street away from my new home just in jeans and the t-shirt. It felt so free, the bike roared and I drove like an asshole through the traffic, buzzing pedestrians, over throttling then rolling off quickly to encourage the backfire. I whizzed through the downtown streets and headed for the waterfront.

The road led me down beneath a building which led me to the seaport. In a world built for cars and trucks, parking a motorcycle, especially without panniers is a breeze. I swung the bike on her side stand, which now lent so far over with the new tires and suspension it looked as if it would fall. I walked down the dock to the floating planes, Johnny stood crisp and white serving the passengers of his aircraft. I was on a high, the marching band was all mine, the bass drum slammed to each heartbeat, and the trumpets trumpeted to each step. I felt grand, not of my actions but in acknowledgement of the world I was in. The horizon boomed from my chest and I smiled from ear to ear.

I walked into the waiting area, full of wealthy Canadians awaiting their flights to their private islands, homes made of thick dark wood, grand art and beautiful views. I checked in and wandered down the pontoon to Johnny, the aircraft was a Beaver, a big single engine up front, sat like a fighter's nose, flat and broad. The wings sat above the fuselage reaching out over the water and pontoon. Placing one hand on the brace I stepped through the small side door into a rather dated and worn interior, utilitarian, like barracks. Johnny let me sit in the co-pilot's seat which elevated the experience, even more, I felt a rising sense of pride for the skills Johnny had gained, his natural breeze of calm sparkled with the technical skills to harness human flight. The seats were narrow and purposeful, a round disc held together the various straps that secured me into the seat and ultimately this giant metal bird. I ran my eyes across the altimeter, a variety of switches labelled pitot heater, magneto, nav lights and ignition. The aircraft was also loaded with post bound for the remote islands, finally three well to-do ladies with deep set tans boarded the rear few seats with the door being secured behind them.

    The plane doors were closed and Johnny began his safety brief. The women listened politely but waited for the monologue that they had obviously heard many times before to finish so they could resume their conversation. I fought the urge to butt in and punch him on the arm and roar with laughter, not that long ago we were confused kids racing boats in Southampton, whilst at university. It was strange how much yet also how little had changed.

    Johnny ran through his checklist of items to prepare for flight. The control surfaces moved freely and the engine kicked into life, Johnny radioed into the Air Traffic Control as we motored out into clear water that would give us long enough run to get airborne. The throttle was compressed fully and the engine roared, even with the headset on the sound overwhelmed the senses, with a few skips on the peaks of waves we were flying, the plane yawed with the cross wind but the air was smooth and within minutes the sea became blue glass as far as the eye could see.

Local flights laws contained us to 1000ft, so out came my camera as I snapped the horizon and beautiful views below. We first headed west out over the bay, over large tankers that had moored in the deeper waters awaiting new crews and destinations. Other tug boats pulled giant floating chains that ensnared hundreds of tonnes of lumber. Fear gripped me as my imagination run wild about being caught amongst the logs as their overwhelming weight would crush the life out of me.

I had flown in small planes before, with Air Cadets and the hours spent on my Private Pilot's License and I had some nightmare moments, from being sick whilst pulling my first loop to being bounced down the airfield on a fast landing. Like small boats at sea, they dance, hop and jig through the air, but Johnny's gyroscopic hands balanced our bird effortlessly as we glided to our first destination.

After the first drop we flew north to Victoria, with precision we swung in between boats moored on the pontoon, all offering the prize of watching orcas and humpbacks in their natural setting, the tourists lined the pontoons with the obligatory technical jackets designed to tackle Everest and functional shoes. I longed for a woman in heels stumbling and sticking between the pontoon slats or someone shivering in shorts and flip flops. To hell with practicality, to hell with it all.

As I walked inland in Victoria, away from the docks I had a movie reel of films circling in my head of orcas hunting like wolf packs, on seals and other sea creatures, and I stood thankful that I wasn't a seal, all cute and blubbery.

Beyond my own gratefulness I thought about humans as a whole, as a species, we have been able to remove ourselves from the food chain, every other animal lives their lives knowing there is a fair chance of being chewed to death by something bigger and more powerful. We still kill each other in droves, maybe this is senseless or maybe this is nature's transformation to keep population in check. Nature's beautiful and mindboggling complexity is something I still need to respect, study, learn from and grow in harmony with, but our intellect should allow us to overcome predisposed behaviours, of violence and define a progressive world. Maybe we will look back at our time and agree we were not the most advanced animal on the planet, merely because we were unable to harmoniously live within our natural world and at the same time push forward with our inherent advantages.

Our only hope is that our collective conscious to work *with* our environment continues to grow and develops into business bottom lines, mainstay ideals and philosophies. Every now and then a human will be mauled to death by a bear or dragged to the depths by a shark. This seems to be little more than other animals flexing their thoughts on us being out of the food chain. Yet our connection to this previous life of survival and constant turmoil is viewed with rose tinted glasses, so we clamber for the lives of beasts and creatures from all angles, yet we seem to learn little.

On Victoria, I walked uphill to the museum, a focal point for the island and which was famed for a capturing the art of the first nations. Totems and elaborate masks stocked the cabinets, all used to describe and understand the world around them, hues of blue, greens and browns covered the bodies of the animal masks, all with large gaping eyes of white and black. Television had destroyed any hope of enjoying this place, everything seemed dated and old, nothing was jumping or screaming at my senses. I would have to read multiple two-dimensional plaques to gather any information on why a stick with feathers on it was important.

I stopped caring, just like I had in any museum I had ever been into. It was time to sit silently in a cafe and stare at my screen, but before I could get there to begin wishing I was somewhere else I had to walk past some old ship that had been torn from its home at sea and placed in this tomb all because it was significant, so said the plaque. When with a thump, whine and a cry a plump child slid down the stairs and lay sobbing on the floor in front of me. I winched him up and sat him on the bottom step. I looked around and no owner seemed to claim him, so I concluded he was clearly sent here to be punished, like a lab testing new antidepressants on a rat. He consoled himself well, clearly through practice, so I let him be. His resilience sparked something in me, combined with my thought of learning from the natural world, I went back to the start of the museum and began to thoroughly read each carefully placed plaque to learn about the land of Victoria. Afterwards I wandered back to the seaport and boarded a plane bound for Vancouver.

I had my motorcycle crated and prepped by Pacific Motosports in Richmond BC, they sold Triumph motorcycles and were honestly the best bunch of grease monkeys I had found so far on this trip. They had received a new batch of Triumph Scramblers a few weeks back and kept one of the factory crates for me. It was free and a perfect fit. I had heard and seen pics of bikes arrive the other end with damage due to the container they were put in, but this was a breeze, the US had very strict rules about shipping things via air that contained fuel. If I had done this from Seattle I would have had to declare this bike a "Highly Hazardous Good" and subjected myself to venomous screening, yet across the border in Canada they required merely less than a quarter tank of fuel and the battery disconnected. I had to unscrew my mirrors and we were set.

Even more conveniently they were just down the road from my cargo company, which was shipping the bike to Incheon in Korea. I spent a few hours packing the bike, taking some pictures and walking around new bikes. All of them looked awful, with their clean and unchipped paint. I considered a midnight raid of the shop to dirty the showroom. Ain't a thing worth nothing without signs of hardship.

I hailed a cab and headed back into town, sitting in a car still felt odd, I leant back in the seat and watched the world pass by. As I drummed a beat on the arm rest and the miles trundled by, the fields which started at the foot of the road gave away to the city limits, and then the steel structures gave way to mountains and snow, which gave away to the sky which gave away its sheen and splendour to God herself. I kept having these grand thoughts of the world around me as each day passed, I was in utter bliss.

I knew someone was looking down on me, and it sure wasn't this shit heel cab driver, with crook teeth and bad odour, coughing his cigarette athleticism over the steering wheel as he screamed obscenities to a woman over the phone. I wished Tina a safe journey and looked forward to seeing her in Korea, yet I was kind of glad to have her tucked away, hidden from my thoughts, I could spin under the sky and not have to factor in tomorrow's ride.

I spent almost a week in Vancouver flying between the islands, drinking, hiking, eating and laughing. From tantalising and delicate Mexican and mystical sushi to hiking the Chief. What a way to end my trip across North America. I had lost myself and forgot the bike. This was largely in part to Johnny and the depth at which we knew each other. This would be a problem ahead, I knew no one to the depth I knew Jonny, and I doubted I would be able to establish anything close to this friendship in the fleeting time that I would stop at each place.

I left North America very proud of Tina, she had cried oil a few times but with a bit of TLC had carried me safely over 5000 miles across mountains, deserts, valleys, plains and highways. At times it did not seem like the easy part of my trip, I was emphatically sad to say goodbye.

I arrived at Vancouver airport early because I was eager to confront my fears of the onward journey into the land of the unknown. I waited patiently in line until it was my turn to approach the desk. I produced my new passport along with my ticket and waited for the questions to begin. It took all of seven minutes until three more staff members were summoned to the desk to help to try to decipher the best course of action for my loose story and poorly photocopied issue of the ferry ticket, which was going to carry me from Seoul to Russia. After a little haggling and some showing off pictures on my phone and my camera I was on my way through and sat in the waiting lounge.

The shipping company had offered the privilege of seeing Tina being loaded onto the aircraft but I declined. I grabbed a cardboard sandwich, sat down, and waited for the boarding to begin. I was calm as a millpond and just really content of what films I could watch whilst I was in the aircraft. Next stop South Korea.

SEOUL

What a wonderful invention, jet propulsion, human flight, pressurised cabins and reclining seats. Only an idiot would embark on a trip like mine when such inventions exist.

The flight was smooth but time stretched as my anxieties grew. On the flight, I found myself sat next to a pretty pale American girl who was heading to Seoul to teach English in a school a couple hours north, not that far from the demilitarised zone. She listened patiently to the synopsis of my trip and asked the diligent questions that so many people had already asked.

Halfway into the flight a melancholy set over me. I felt ever so lonely and to cover myself I pretended to be half asleep letting my hand fall from the armrest onto her thigh, we caught eye contact but said nothing but a smile. Her warmth was resonating through her jeans, comforting me and soon I was in a deep sleep. I was woken by the ping of the seatbelt sign being turned on and the approach into Seoul and just like that I was South Korea.

I took a bus into downtown Seoul, on the ride in my melancholy left as I remembered I had two friends flying in to join me for a few days in Korea. My bike was to be delivered the following day. I had been dealing with a lady, who had been recommended to me by another traveller that used her to get his bike from South Korea to Vancouver. Her resourcefulness had been astonishing, I spent time thinking about what she might look like as I had only spoken with her over email. Yet I trusted her implicitly with Tina.

The buildings of Seoul soon rose through windows of the bus, just like London, they stood tall from the earth, desperate to impress but the dirt of combustion had masked their sheen, revealing the city's price it was failing to pay. Wealth was clear but city planning was not, each enterprise begged for attention through loud print on white banners and neon signs. Through a European's eye the message was lost and had become a piece of the next photograph rather than an enticement to visit someone's enterprise. Like many Asian cultures a dichotomy exists with the west where we aspire to be an entrepreneur, a self-sustained made man, yet here everyone runs their own business, whether that be the owning of a small nimble truck or access to exotics goods, everyone appears to wheel and deal their way to an income.

I checked into my hotel room, after dropping off my bags and a hot shower and I went down to the lobby where I waited for my friends Willis and John to arrive. They'd arranged to meet me here when I was planning the trip in Boston, I was overly eager to meet a friendly face.

Whilst I sat in the lobby I received a call from the shipping company, I could have the bike delivered to my hotel tonight, for an extra $100. I jumped at the chance.

Willis and John arrived via Tokyo that evening, after a big hug and shared smiles we crossed the road and sat in a simple bar overlooking the hotel, this way I could see when the truck arrived carrying Tina. I was nervous to see what state she would arrive, for the last 24 hours she had been held in a metal crate in the unpressurized hold of the aircraft all the way from Vancouver, handled by hands unknown. A small white flatbed truck pulled up outside the hotel and out popped a man with paperwork in his hand looking confused on where to go. I bound towards him with giant steps created by my six-foot-two frame. He wielded back against the truck door as I stopped next to him. I didn't know any Korean, so I did the universal symbol for motorcycles, which was outstretched arms with fists clenched palms facing down and a twist of the right wrist yelling engine noises of vroom vroom. He smiled back and let down the side panels of his truck exposing the crate containing Tina. As the curtains unfolded and she stood there in the exact same condition I left her some 3000 miles ago in Vancouver. I couldn't believe my luck. I gave the delivery driver a massive hug, Willis proceeded to jump into the back of the truck, placing hands on the pannier racks and tried to move the bike. I leant back and laughed loudly as he underestimated the girth of Tina. "Looks like CrossFit isn't enough." I laughed.

 John stood beside me with a beer in his hand watching the proceedings. Willis couldn't move it, and that the truth was all three of us couldn't move it together, Tina was a brute, all metal and hulk, the truck stood some four feet from the road and we needed to devise a plan. The hotel was positioned on a side street so we walked out onto the main road. I looked around for a wooden plank or large piece of metal that I could use to leveraged the bike off or at least roll it down. However, the street wasn't equipped to handle offloading motorcycles from the back of trucks, so we had to take a different plan, one that involved bribery. Stood on the brow of the hill was a group of seven or eight teenage lads. John knew a little Korean so he became the point man for this endeavour.

With several six packs under our arms and a mix of broken Korean and English, we were able to convince the guys to come and help unload Tina from the back of the truck. With ten of us in total, the task was heavily over staffed but became a fun team event and a very simple hop to the road. The tires had barely touched the ground when I whipped out my toolkit. I reconnected the fuel, the battery, wing mirrors and reattached the seat. With that done I put the key in the ignition. This was going to be the true test to see if she had survived. I turned the key to the first notch, the lights came on, I turned the key to the second notch, the engine turned over. Half a second passed and the engine roared into life. I smiled and opened the throttle all the way screaming the engine, people covered their ears and my smile grew louder, everything was groovy. I swung Tina into the underground garage that accompanied the hotel and we headed out into town. By this point, the sun had set leaving nothing but the night to illuminate the neon streets. Willis, as always, had done copious amounts of research on where to go and what to see, making the night such a breeze. I was just along for the ride, no decision was mine to make and I was happy for the fact.

It was 2 a.m. and I had my face pressed against the glass of a taxi window, watching the lights fly by as we headed to our next waypoint. We headed down to the garment district, a place that was notorious for partying late into the night. Like a giant neon fish, this area of Seoul never stopped moving. Hundreds of men and boys pushed trolleys loaded ten feet high with boxes of clothes and fabrics, moving effortlessly around each other and the narrow streets.

We found a restaurant that bordered the garment district, makeshift and simple, built out of a few 2x4 frames covered with thin waxed cotton that acted as protection from the elements. I was tired and running on adrenaline. I watched bleary-eyed as countless little plates arrived on our plastic table.

We repeated this for 4 consecutive nights of 7 a.m. bedtimes, with amazing food arriving in dishes no bigger than ash trays, served fifteen at a time, all with different flavours of red and spice, textures of crisp and smooth, velvet and snap.

Like a beautiful house viewed fleetingly through trees, the intricacies of the world can only be seen if the speed was slow enough, yet the last few nights were at the speed of light and little could be remembered let alone learnt.

It was time to head out of Seoul and head towards the East coast. My wheels took me North as Willis and Jon followed behind with their hire car, towards the Demilitarized Zone (DMZ). Our visit was at a time when the Northern leader was trying to prove himself a man, causing high tensions between the north and south, we found ourselves passing humongous tanks smoking deep black smoke, patrolling the Southern border, forcing us to weave and dive out of the way as they squeezed their way through tunnels and passes.

The rain abated just as we arrived at the DMZ allowing us to see the so-called "forbidden land", an old bullet-riddled train from the Korean war sat there showing the force and might of war in the twisted and blasted and hurt iron and steel. We snapped a few pics and decided to continue moving east. The routes were kind even though we had to stay away from the motorways due to restrictions placed on motorcycles, navigation wasn't too difficult and the interior was stunning with dense swallow green hills and mountains.

We arrived in the small coastal fishing town of Sockcho, known for its raw fish a little after 3pm, the town covered no more than ten square miles until it hit the Sea of Japan. John had booked us into a hotel that gave some colour to the grey skies droning in from the sea. We pulled into the car park that sat at the foot of the Korean version of the Adams Family Home. Spires and grand windows reached north into the sky with grand marble steps, the walls were painted green and the doors tattered on their hinges opened to more marble and a reception desk hidden behind extra thick Perspex, then metal bars, with a small dome cut at the bottom to exchange whatever items this hotel served.

We were promptly asked how many hours we needed, to which I responded how many hours are in a Korean night, we paid the amount for the respective rooms and proceeded up the ornate stairwell, we agreed an hour was sufficient to freshen up and head into town for dinner.

Upon opening my room, I was confronted with a large round orange bed with a pink plastic stand next to it containing various body lotions and oils. Still holding all my bags, I walked into a plastic green bathroom to realise there was a one-way mirror from the bathroom overlooking the bed, tonight I'd be in my sleeping bag as the prospect of waking up stuck to the sheets was not something I wanted to entertain.

I jumped in a taxi with the others and headed down to walk around the hand painted one story town, the largest and most noticeable of buildings was the blue fish market, where huge octopus fought in tubs, their tentacles reaching through the netting covering the tanks, huge gutted fish hung from their tails from rusted blue hooks, water was constantly being pumped into the various containers, overflowing onto the ground and around your feet, the assault on the senses was brilliant.

We all got excited about the evening's dinner at one of the many seafood restaurants, the only challenge now was to choose one. We finally settled on a busy place with a picture of the owner on the sign. We were ushered to the tables with chairs but asked to sit on the shorter, more traditional tables that required you to sit on the floor, a novel idea that soon wore off as my bony behind started hurting ten minutes in, a distraction to the pain soon arrived when our order of fish was delivered to the table, it looked like Sole, yet prepared in a way I had never seen before, the top of the fish was cut into domino-size pieces and tasted delightful, after four or five mouthfuls I looked down to see the mouth of the fish move, I blinked and froze as I saw it move again. You couldn't argue with the freshness.

We finished the meal and looked for the next source of entertainment, little seemed to move in the night, so we hit a corner store for some alcohol and headed back to the hotel. On the walk up the hill, we saw a store selling fireworks, perfect for the hotel carpark. Willis stood back as me and Kirst fired rockets at one another and anything that seemed like a good target, the lamp post, a sign, a tree, our full NATO assault was brought short when the owner of the only car in the carpark screamed from his bedroom window about sparks that were raining down on his paintwork. What we hadn't realised was that the wind was carrying the sparks down around the corner, peppering his car.

Upon sunrise, on the following day, we headed to a national park just south of where we were staying and I was keen to stretch my legs and work a sweat. We did a short hours hike to a small waterfall that lay a few clicks up a deep gorge. The waterfall fell in a rather unimpressive way to a small pool but the change from the road was welcome. Next, we rode in a cable car rising high above the clouds that started our final hike to an amazing peak that presented forest and mountain views across Korea, it was a beautiful sight of greys and blues as far as the eye could see. Back down in the carpark we said our goodbyes as I left Willis and Kirst to return to Seoul to catch their flight home.

I arrived at the port Donghae, the port from which I would catch my ship to Russia, as I stood there preparing the bike, it hit me like a punch to the back, lurching me forward, having Willis and John by my side I had forgotten the trip enough to keep me present and centred, maybe this would be the state I was in if the trip were over several years not months, I still shuddered at the thought of being away for such a length of time but I was starting to question my defences to that idea, maybe I could wander until the end of time. It takes me a while to tune into the beauty of a place, London's beauty is held with the back streets and offbeat institutions of science, so much has come from that city it is simply staggering. Boston's beauty is the water, and the food it holds, I found beautiful fishmongers that were stocked full of sweet oysters, bass and lobster. To harmonise with a diversity as large as a city it takes time, now I was taking on the world and I was realising that 3 months would never be enough, would even a lifetime?

All I knew was that the world seemed less daunting when I had buddies with me, and now they were gone and I was back with my thoughts. I felt optimistic and fragile.

I cleared the paperwork checks with a little push and was told to leave my bike on the dock edge until it was my turn to wheel her on board. Few trucks or cars occupied the hold as I worked with a greasy kid to secure the bike. The room would be locked shut once we were out at sea so I left the main luggage attached to the bike and took the essentials to keep me happy and legal if I had to swim to shore. Just as I reached the door I took one look back and realised I might need my sleep kit, so I quickly unhooked the bags as the boat sounded its horn and grumbled away from the concrete pillars.

I became indestructible in this foreign land simply with the presence of two friends that were not related to me in any other way than we worked at the same company. Humans are the ultimate pack animal, yet now I was alone and heading to far eastern Russia.

SEA OF JAPAN

I sat crossed legged on a top bunk of our eight-bunk room watching the other men fill their beds. Each bunk was shrouded in tragic gold curtains, they sat like lipstick on a rat catchers dog. They weren't long enough to conceal the whole bed so a decision had to be made and it was my feet I'd put on display to the world. At the back of the room sat a growling extraction fan working with all its strength to draw the musk of five bodies.

Our crew was the old jar in a workshop, full of odd bolts and nuts. To my right were two British men, with a private school ease, backpacking around the world in their old button down oxford cloth, below them was a short and broad Korean man that did nothing but sleep and clip his toenails whilst eating secretively from a plastic bag. Near the door a well fed Russian who held himself with a gentle care and a brimming sweetness behind the crook teeth, pitted skin and long hair. He explained through stories of old records and motorcycles he had a shop in downtown Vladivostok. His name was Yureg. Together we made Room 1203.

I laid on my back with the curtain drawn tugging the pull chain to the light in sync with a loud clang that rang through the ship's bulkhead every few seconds. I had nothing to kill but time. I wanted something to write about so I pulled the curtain back to this listen to the stories of the room only to realise everyone had left except the Korean, who was, as for the majority of this trip, asleep with his back to the room. A cold sweetness rushed through my body. I quickly stored my kit and walked the ship to find the draw of everyone onboard. It was food time. A chaotic food hall paraded erratically with the Russian chatter that signalled like a flare bright into the ocean night I was storming towards another world to explore, consume and be terrified.

Occupying the time at sea was easier to accomplish than I had previously anticipated. I had forgotten to get my Rubles hidden in the panniers up to the cabin and now we were out at sea the hold was firmly locked down. So I was going hungry, this was a problem. I honestly believe my mind burns more calories than physical activities, and right at this moment this fucker was in overdrive with what lay ahead. Siberia, Trans-Siberian highway, Haruhisa Watanabe, the guy who was killed doing the same route as me twelve months' prior, sustaining fatal injuries after being hit by a large truck and every other fucking possibility. Therefore, I had to get creative to not only calm my fears but to give me energy for what lay ahead.

Escapades set in motion a fantastic scavenger hunt on board a Korean ship in the Sea of Japan heading for Far Eastern Russia, tell no more for it was here to believe, what a fucking adventure. However, a master sleuth I am not. So stale bread stolen from the food hall, which in hindsight was probably free, became my most prized possession. Combined with Bovril, I was in heaven. I sat there with my legs crossed partially covered by my tattered golden veil grinning feverously as the black tar sank into the cracks, wondrous stuff.

After my feed I headed out to the rear deck. Looking out to sea, the endless constant, no future or past just the present as far as the eyes can see. Bright fresh air brought a smile to my face. I couldn't lie, I was nervous, I wanted answers to the blackness that sat beyond the horizon, on the shores of Russia. The country seemed cold to an outsider, desolate towns run by corrupt politicians, with sparse grey faces of stoicism and aggression.

Yureg's prized GPS indicated we were about 70kms from Vladivostok, at our current speed we would be in the dock in a few hours, I readied my bags and sat watching the others gather their things. I was ready to get off the boat and see what was around.

The boat docked and everyone headed to the gang walk to exit down to the harbourside. I turned tail and walked towards the hold to retrieve Tina and ride to my hotel, a bed that I could lay straight out in would be a delightful prize.

I waited by the door yet no one came. I walked the corridors for a bit and no one seemed to be around, so I left the same way everyone had gone and walked along the blue harbour wall to the rear of the ship. There I found a Russian in blue and grey coveralls standing in large clumsy work boots on the bottom of the boarding ramp. I pointed in Tina's direction, twisting my wrist full throttle whilst pointing at myself with the other hand. He pointed me to another man stood under a small porch, he was much younger than the other guy yet he held a clipboard. I walked over with a smile.

'One week,' he said.

I tried to explain that I was here to collect my motorcycle.

'One week, paperwork takes one week.'

What was "fuck!" in Russian?

FAR EASTERN RUSSIA

Luckily, I had decided to grab my bags before leaving the bike else I would be sleeping rough until my bike was released. Whilst stood there thinking of the best way to solve the problem a Dutch man appeared at my side, with vanishing hair and odd tan lines he was clearly on a bike. He explained to me that he was also waiting for his bike and that Russian processing was so inefficient that a week is usual to get your bike from the boat, but he had been told there was a guy that could help expedite the issue in town and he had scheduled a meeting with him tomorrow. Soon Yureg was at my side and confirmed Dutch's comments. So we planned all to meet tomorrow morning.

I jumped in a cab and headed to the Hotel. Vladivostok or "Vlad" as the locals would say, looked like the love child of Marseilles and unhappiness. Once at the hotel, I bedded down and relaxed instantly into a deep sleep until the early hours came round. I walked down the metal staircase on the outside of the hotel that led from my room, it dropped me behind two huge steel gates that hid the hotel and the steam rooms below.

I met Yureg and Dutch and we headed up the hill to meet the man with the skills - by skills I mean we pay a guy to expedite a process that should take five minutes.

Orthodox Christian chapels, Lutheran churches, German Gothic and Romanesque, intricate Russian Baroque and Asian architecture were everywhere. This place once held a grandeur, bold and strong with Communist might, but many buildings sat like defeated heavyweight champions, their legs sprawled out in front of them with windows missing and boarded doors.

We arrived at a steel door that ran alongside a workshop and a breakers yard. We entered into a large room full of dark-haired men holding paper, just like the ones me and Dutch held. Only a few of the twenty or so had had a shave, the amount of men that there were staring blankly into infinity filled me with content, I wasn't the only one going through this racket. We spoke to our man, some money changed hands and I was informed Tina would be by my side on Wednesday, five days earlier than what I'd been told at the port.

I sorted my accommodations for the following few nights by moving into a half dome hotel that was painted white, it stood near the shore on the east part of town. Summer retreats with caviar and vodka were long gone, as the paint peeled from the walls and the decor hung unchanged on the 300 plus rooms. I hauled, unpacked and secured my luggage, it was too hot for jeans and I needed some shorts. It was far warmer than I had anticipated so I headed to the town square, I was soon stood at a rack of shorts folding and rolling them to check their packability. I was able to find a pair with my initials on, Physical Education; they were also the only pair that wasn't adorned with the Saint Georges Cross or the Union Flag.

Once correctly attired, I found a local store that had the ingredients for a tasty ploughman's, albeit without a pickled onion. I walked down the waterfront until I made the main square. At first, I thought nothing of it as I had forgotten where I was, but as I walked on and I saw another, I stopped and looked back. It was the US Navy, in full dress, snapping pics along the Vladivostok waterfront. As I walked further, more servicemen and women from the US appeared and the crowds grew until we were all in the square and could barely move due to throng of people. The square was pretty standard by anyone's assessment, with its fountain in the middle, ornate lamp posts and checkered tiling. I perched on a wall that separated the square and the beach some twenty feet below and started at my lunch. As I chomped down into the bread and ham, doughnuts of people started to gather around a single person, three of these human donuts now occupied the square some ten meters between one another. In the centre of the doughnuts sat a commonality, it was an African American, being treated with novelty and reverence. People waited patiently with large grins with their cell phones at the ready to have their photos taken with them.

 The sun now half way through it cycle caused me to make my way back down to the town centre. It was the Saint George Parade, orange and black ribbon, a different George than ours but a George nonetheless. This was the first show of the Russian power, strength, and menace I had seen many military parades yet compared to British parades it all seemed a little a sadder and it was the first time I encountered the Russian Drunk. What a force. An all-consuming belligerence of reckless abandonment, a professional career and a wonderful collapse on helpless bliss. Men on their own littered the streets, on benches and on arms of the local police, being dragged merrily down alleyways to presumably a large pile of more drunks, like disorganised sardines, stacked on top of one another. The men grew long and childish in their vodka dreams. One brute looked like he had reached some sort of Nirvana, childish eyes and a gimpy grin sat subconsciously on his face, yet a terror lurked somewhere in these men, their muscles were grown and cut, crimes yet unanswered.

I watched many jostle and coerce like winter waves on the shore, one nonchalantly pushed three policemen to the floor and staggered on until the three policemen finally overpowered him. To the drunk it was all a game. Everywhere else the crowd cheered the soldiers marching next to their large murder machines. A ribbon was forced into my hand by a middle-aged woman, the ribbon of Black and Orange, I yelled at her as she moved on.

'What does it mean?'

She yelled back in Russian as she disappeared into the cloud, I later found out it stood for good luck. I collected Tina the following day and prepared to head out. Tina was running smoothly, all the fluid was where it needed to be and we were away. My biggest fear was the road, there were thousands of miles to cover and constant reports of vast stretches of road deteriorating into sand, gravel and dirt and hardship. I was ready for the fight but I was scared.

Heading north from Vladivostok I planned to ride the 750 km to Khabarovsk in one go. The road started well as a paved and smooth two-lane motorway, it continued like this for quite a distance and then out of nowhere the road disappeared. In its place was a wide strip of wet, loose and thick gravel and stones that went on for as far as the eye could see. The cars barely slowed as they bounced and jumped through the water filled pot holes. I, on the other, slowed down to almost 10 miles per hour as the bike snaked under her own weight. The tires slipped and slid in the gravel, in a panic I opened the throttle fully, lurching the bike forwards. My feet cartwheeled off the pegs and lifted in front of me. I slowed the bike to bring it under control, somehow I'd managed to stay upright.

The road continued to change in three very distinct ways over the next eleven hours of riding. From smooth asphalt to deep gravel then consecutive speed bumps, similar to large corrugated iron sheets that would bounce the bike like a bull in a rodeo if you rode too fast. This was what it was about, being outside my comfort zone, but being there and getting through it, like any good fight, I had to go beyond what I knew to find a deeper realm of knowledge of my fingers and heart and sinew and courage and tears and dirt and Tina.

I found my groove at thirty to forty miles per hour and sometimes up to sixty, then my vision would be so blurred and the bike bucking so hard I'd scare myself back down to ten. The surrounding views remained constant or so I remember. Transfixed on the road ahead the world blinkered away, like mountaineering, I became so transfixed on my line, gear placement, foot placement and hand holds that the galaxy of beauty I was operating in ceased to exist. Until my lungs burnt too much or my muscles became solid, being forced to stop. Only then does the world wash in. On the bike, fuel caused me to stop every 120 miles or so. My fear of fuel station scarcity was unfounded and I paid mostly on my credit card. Tina kept chugging along as the Boreal Forrest finally started to grow and maintain itself alongside the road all the way to Khabarovsk.

    I was starting to learn, my hands were relaxing, the bike glided on, when out of nowhere the road become racetrack asphalt. I roared the engine open and away we moved, I took my feet off the pegs and laid out on the bike in a superman position, it opened my hips and air rushed through cracks in my jacket there were previously hidden, I exhaled and smiled for what felt like the first time that day.

    Traffic continued to whiz past at Mach-10 with some near hits and close calls but I chugged on with glory inside and the adventure under me. I caught sight of a large dump truck approaching in my mirror, so my muscles slowed the bike a little and I moved close to the verge as this large hulk of metal came to pass. Its load of rubble created a sandstorm in its wake, for a full ten seconds I could not see past my front wheel, yet before I could slow down the bike I was in the air, my stomach hit the back of my throat. The road had ended and dropped some ten inches down into sand and gravel. My heart didn't stop, it shut down, left my arse and was waiting in line for its flight home. The rear of the bike hit the sand and whipped hard left then right and left, the front wheel turned hard right causing me to muscle it straight. I must have been going sixty miles per hour. I used my legs as keels and the bike righted itself. We came to stop in a plume of dust and flying gravel. I looked around, no one was there.

The truck was long gone and I was okay, I turned the throttle and pulled away.

About a hundred and fifty kilometres short of my destination many motorcycles heading in the same direction started to pass me. They zipped over the gravel and sand with such ease I couldn't help but be envious but I knew this was their stomping ground, their bread and butter. At my final petrol station, I met two brothers, Nikolai and Sergey, whereby they explained that it was the opening of the bike season for the Far East of Russia in Khabarovsk, an annual event where riders from all over congregated to celebrate their two-wheeled freedom machines. It brought back great memories of home, the sense of community that bikes bring, the honest and strange characters they attract. They said there was room at the small house they were staying at so I followed them into town where we met up with a plethora of more Russian bikers.

We congregated at the city limits, as more and more bikers joined. My favourites were two petite girls on a 250cc Baja Scrambler who seemed madly in love with one another, with their torn army jackets, shit kicker boots and delicate cheekbones they eased the crowd and my heart, taking turns to sit on each other laps. On the other end of the spectrum of riders was an Americanized Harley rider, he went by the nickname "Doctor" and was very round only in the gut area, elsewhere he seemed almost skinny. He quickly took me under his wing as we continued on to our lodgings. We arrived at a set of long buildings that were soviet era summer camps for children, now abandoned and used yearly by local and travelling bikers. Doctor proudly showed me around the camp where a courtyard held trodden grass, cracked concrete and a brand new wooden gazebo which was home to a coal-fired grill. These guys had their priorities straight. The building was one story and ran for about two hundred meters along the foot of a small grass hill. Inside the repetition of white and grey rooms one after another, same in size and shape became my home for the next two nights.

My room, just as all the others, consisted of two soviet era children's beds, five feet long and two and a half feet wide, which was somewhat confusing as all around me were very tall men and women, like British oak. They must have had some soviet gene that stunted or withheld growth until a certain age. The other bed in my room was already occupied with an old, tall, withdrawn Russian with a permanent look of childish fear in his eyes. He was dressed in old jeans and a tattered black leather jacket over a blue and white stripped t-shirt. At first, I thought he was a worker at the summer camp but it later turned out he was part of the crowd and rode a big KTM.

I sat on the bed watching him sleep as I tried to organize my kit, not knowing what to feel about the situation. I was glad to meet some other Sapiens, everyone had been kind and generous, heartfelt and warm. Yet in the back of my psyche, I did not trust them, I had no reason to doubt their souls or actions or words, but I was very far from home and the language created a ravine that would take some time to traverse and cross. Everything around me seemed depleted and dying. People would stare at me with stoic eyes that fronted a life of which I had no knowledge. Would reading about this part of the world alleviate this feeling? Who knows, it was too late and I was here. I was on the cliff of a new chapter, thousands of feet into the air, high above the clouds. All I had to do was spread my arms, close my eyes and lean until gravity took hold but what was beneath the clouds?

I had a wash with a wet wipe and went back outside to let myself relax to a couple shots of vodka and some delicious borscht.

We sat out under the wooden gazebo letting the sun set as they explained the plan for the following day's activities in broken English. I had planned to ride on the following day but the Doctor asked if I would stay and join them in the motorcycle parade that routed itself through the town centre. He explained there would be some two hundred bikers going, I agreed and headed for the pillow. As I let my body go to sleep I noted how loving everyone was, albeit in a stern, terrifying kind of way.

The following morning, I awoke to rain and black skies as we headed out in a twelve-person convoy to the start of the parade. I had anticipated a short ride down to the local square and a few circles of the central streets, however, we rode for nearly sixty miles to a car park in an adjoining town. On the way to the parade, a taxi driver had reversed into one of the bikers, he must have been travelling all of ten miles per hour, but what ensued was my introduction to the Siberian Car Insurance Business. The taxi driver got out of his cab, the biker kept his helmet on and walked towards him, he had lowered his chin and his fists were clenched. The taxi drive had nothing to protect him other than his six foot eight inches and shovel hands. Words were exchanged between the biker and the driver and then began a full on fist brawl, heavy punches landing on the cheek, chin and eye with quick succession. Two further bikers joined in until the driver hit the ground. As soon as he was down, that was it, insurance details had been exchanged. My stomach turned in somersaults, I was scared of any repercussions to what had happened to the driver.

We arrived at the start of the parade which was a large gated car park that filled with nearly five hundred bikes. Word quickly spread of a foreigner riding solo around the world and many people came to have their picture taken with me, or have their child sit on my bike with me stood behind. The attention was bizarre but pleasant. After lunch I was approached by a Russian TV station wanting to do an interview. I explained I didn't speak any Russian but would try my best to explain what I was doing. I was able to stretch out a five-minute hand puppet explanation of my adventure and why I was doing it, the reason I gave I can no longer remember.

We completed the parade back in town and headed towards the camp with my bunch of misfits. They rode aggressively through crazy traffic at high speeds, it unsettled me as I didn't know the way back to the camp and was keen to keep up. A small white van darted in front of me causing me to brake hard, my front wheel slipped out from under me on the wet gravel, my foot caught under the bike as Tina and I slid down the road. I came to a stop and took two breaths. I searched my body in my mind for sources of pain but none came.

I pulled myself from under the bike and switched the ignition off. One of the other riders stopped and helped me right my bike. My fuel canister had snapped off and was left hanging on the straps holding the bags, a large dent resided in one of the panniers and I had torn my jacket quite badly on the shoulder and elbow.

Adrenaline coursed through my body, I looked around and sat back on my bike. I felt small and embarrassed to what had happened, a stupid mistake riding my bike well beyond what the environment allowed. Lesson learnt.

We arrived back at the camp to find the Russian profession flowing with copious quantities. Voda is the word for water in Russian, they use the letter K to shorten words, so Vodka literally translates as 'little water'. It might explain why they drink so much of the stuff. I planned to leave early the following morning so sobriety became my main focus. I had to duck and dive away from the constant shots of vodka being handed to me which in Russia was a sign of good luck for a long journey. I kept a glass of water with me at all times that I could easily cheer, keep them happy and me upright, a great trick.

The Bikers poured in until the place was overrun. Large groups formed and fists started swinging. A thuggish society can be judged by the number of women with broken noses, I counted thirteen. Large hunting knives were compared as I was ushered away from a group who readily carried guns. I stayed close to Sergey and enjoyed the world spinning round me.

At 10pm I quietly disappeared to my room to allow the day's events to sink in and to let my heart rate slow. My roommate was nowhere to be seen, so I sat down on his bed and laid out all my kit in front of me on my bed for the following day. The shallow drum of singing, fighting and laughing continued outside. All of a sudden my door became consumed by a large figure holding a bottle of vodka, staring at me with wide blank eyes. He wore fifty years under a tattered shirt and bike trousers. I stood quickly moving towards him, a hand outstretched to shake.

'I'm Paul, Motocicle, round the world,' I said, circling with my finger.

He batted my hand away with the back of his, coupled with a slur of Russian words, my heart truly sank, what was going to happen next? I sat back down on the bed and started rummaging through my bags searching to find my GPS so I could show him my route, hoping it would clearly explain my purpose and give me acceptance. The five minutes he stood there felt like fifty, he did not utter a word. With two large steps he was by my side where he turned and collapsed on my bed, straight into a deep, snoring sleep. I sat there feeling his stomach move in and out on my lower back, simply too scared to move. I hoped the incident was merely a communication breakdown, but my gut instinct said to move. I reached out and grabbed all my belongings and walked down the hall. Finding an empty room I threw all my stuff down and locked the door behind me by pulling a small set of draws across the door.

I slept well and was on the bike at 6a.m. heading towards Svobodny, to stay with one of my new friend's best mates, a bike mechanic and avid biker.

The day started off well with fair weather and a solid footing beneath the bike, the petrol stations came up just as I needed them, the kindness of the Russian pump attendants was a welcome break, again they seemed quietly curious on what I was doing and seemed to go out of their way to help me out. The second half of the day tested me as the road broke down to wet mud. I came to rest at the head of a dirt track, my GPS suggested I go left, down a trail. So left I went, leaving behind the very rare Siberian commodity of smooth asphalt. I was close to completing the day's ride of nearly eight hundred kilometres and I was tired, eyes drawing closed and the cold rang from the inside out making my muscles tense and my spine ache.

The dirt track was about twenty feet wide edged by small pines, the road was made of mud but it seemed fairly dry as far as I could see. I was in the zone and gave no thought to the idea that this was the wrong track and that a brand new road, all smooth and paved, sat a kilometre round the bend that led down into Svobodny, the town where I'd be staying that night. I looked back over my shoulder, twisted and started down the track. The mud was wetter than it looked and the bike squirmed readily as I went. I pushed the throttle further and stood up onto the balls of my feet with Tina straightening her tail. We trundled on down the track when, without a thought,

Tina stopped dead as the front wheel sunk three-quarters into a thick glue.

I pitched forward and, with no effort from me, was flying over the handle bars. I didn't even have time to extend my arms as I flew through the air. My headphones were yanked down through my helmet as my head hit the dirt and my body cartwheeled after. I slid forward on my back for another twenty feet before my heels sunk in, flipping me to my front where I came to rest face down in the thick honey mud. I laid there waiting for some pain receptors to fire. I focused my thoughts on my left foot, then my other, then my arms and shoulders, spine, wrists and chest. Nothing came back, I was fine.

I pushed myself up and looked down my body, over the dirt packed trousers to Tina. She sat on her side, covered in mud. Further back, I could see one of my panniers and both of my bags, I made my way over to the bike and righted her. I went to push her to the side of the road but I couldn't get her out of gear as the gear shifter had bent flat against the crankcase. My clothes were heavy and cold with all the extra mud, with everything weighed down it was a struggle to hump Tina to the side of the track. With her upright, I collected my panniers and saw that the hooks that held them to the frame were snapped off. I put all my bags in a neat pile on the other side of the track opposite the bike and looked around. I took a quick stroll making sure nothing else lay hid in the mud. I went back over to Tina and tried to get her started again, nothing came.

The evening started closing in, with little cloud cover the day's warmth quickly dissipated. An hour or so passed when up the track came three men. I could see they were all staggering heavily. My heart sank; all three wore cold faces and filthy clothes. Blondie, the one in the middle, stood quite a bit taller and broader, he held a bottle of Vodka and it was nearly empty. The other two looked like brothers, dark haired with hard eyes. The one on the right held a broad scar running from his ear lobe down the side of his neck. All three wore only jeans and a t-shirt yet the cold did nothing to bother them. For some reason, my thoughts flashed back to the drunken Russian the night before, who gate crashed my room. I tensed. They muttered amongst themselves as they staggered straight to my pile of bags and panniers on the other side of the track. They had not spoken a single word or even a nod in my direction but the pile of bags and boxes seemed to intrigue them immensely. They discussed what was at their feet for a solid ten minutes before turning to walk in my direction.

I was still a little dazed from the crash and had stayed silent just watching them inspect my goods. I moved in close next to Tina. I knew I had my phone, wallet and passport on me. As they approached they still remained ignorant to the fact I was even there, eyeing up Tina. One of the brothers with jet black hair was now holding the bottle and Blondie attempted to get onto my bike, missing the seat with his leg a couple of times before finally coming to rest on the saddle. I looked down and saw the keys still in the ignition. He fumbled at the controls searching for what I presumed was the ignition switch, after a moment, he finally found it. He turned her over, my heart stopped. The engine failed to catch. My heart started beating again.

I waved my hands in front of him so he would stop. As delicately as the Vodka would allow him, he batted me away and mumbled something in Russian. I noticed his hands were just like his shoulders, broad and flat. He put his hand into his pocket where he produced an old flip phone. He smacked it around with his large sausage like fingers, maybe he was calling someone to collect his Christmas presents. Whatever he was doing put me further on edge, whether he was about to beat me with it or call for more thugs, he handed me the phone with a blurry video paused and ready to play. I still hadn't uttered a word. He tapped the air, huffing at me to start the video clip. I stood and watched a movie of a bare-knuckle boxer bloodying his opponent as other men cheered and screamed, Blondie was tapping himself on his chest with his finger, speaking slowly in Russian. I pointed back at him to acknowledge who it was, with a clenched fist, he nodded. This was getting better and better.

Blondie sat on my bike as one of the dark haired brothers staggered around swigging deeply from the remains of the bottle. The third man appeared at my side and thrust me his phone. This time, there was no video playing but a connected call. He tossed his head up a couple of times for me to speak, I pushed the phone up between my helmet. I waited, no one spoke.

'Hello?' I questioned.

'Hello, are you ok?' a woman asked.

'Yeah...'

'I'm Demetri's old English teacher and he says you need help?'

'Yeah…' I squeaked again.

My mind flipped one hundred and eighty degrees, I was simply lost for words.

'Don't worry about these men,' she continued 'They are here to help you and will look after you.'

'I am staying with a motorcycle mechanic in Svobodny.'

'You mean Svet?'

'Yes, him,' I blurted.

I was so happy she knew the stranger I was staying with.

'Stay there, we will be with you soon.'

The call ended and I took my helmet off, allowing the air in my lungs to finally exit. Within thirty minutes a red pick-up truck was by my side, driven by Svet. The English teacher sat in the passenger seat. Within minutes the bike was loaded and we were heading into town.

We made our way back to Svet's house via his workshop which was a large concrete box, just like the four others on either side. Each box was fronted by a large steel door that was fastened to the box by two large lift off hinges. Each steel door had a smaller door cut into the bottom left near the main hinges. Svet's smaller door was badly beaten and didn't close properly. Someone, probably Svet, had fashioned a lock by drilling a hole large enough to hold the huge metal chain and padlock. Many scars engraved the door but all were welded over and taken care of. We backed the pickup to the main door and offloaded Tina into the workshop.

Inside, the shop was almost pitch black, minus small cracks of light shining in around the door frames. There appeared to be no windows in the box. As the lights flickered on, an array tools and mess appeared, on top of a thick oiled ground with dotted engines, cranks, drive trains, clutches and frames. In the far back was a makeshift room created with breeze blocks and plasterboard. It was spotless and well lit, the complete opposite to the rest of the shop. There, in the centre of this white room, stood a KTM Dakar. Svet stood there beaming at his pride and joy. We talked about his adventures to northern Siberia on this bike through hand actions.

We made our way back outside, as two mechanics worked on an old BMW estate and an old potbellied man with a once white vest re-welded an ornate iron gate. The nine boxes sat in a concrete square broken by grass, roots and time, circled by soviet era housing blocks. The housing blocks stood fifteen apartments high and twenty or so long. The buildings were soul-sapped with Russian utilitarianism, wood and glass evenly sharing most of the window frames. I jumped back into the pickup and left Tina. We turned right onto the main road which was heavily pitted and beaten.

The beaten roads of Boston I had so readily noticed a month or so ago appeared like Silverstone to where I was being driven now. Svet swung the car left and right to avoid the potholes, sometimes coming full wing onto the opposing side of the road. Oncoming traffic agreeably moved and everyone continued along in this organised chaos all the way back to Svet's house. The house sat on about an acre of land, with a single roomed house to the right, a corrugated plastic parking bay that sat in front of a small allotment, a small barn and an outhouse. I lugged my things inside the house and took off my mud-caked clothes, being careful not to spill mud all over their quaint little home. The kitchen consisted of a wood fired stove next to a trolley, which held a basin. The water must have come from a well nearby. A plastic pink curtain separated the kitchen from the lounge which happened to double as my bedroom. Svet's wife was in the kitchen chopping potatoes and boiling water on the stove, she stood a little taller than Svet but just as lean and welcoming. Her short brown hair reminded me of my mother's and she held a confident smile as she stared at me and ran the knife over the potato with ease. I was ushered to sit down.

 Svet's English was better than his wife's, although I struggled to make her name, I gave up asking him to repeat after the third attempt and resided to not knowing. They stood side-by-side looking at me as I felt my body relax into the home. I counted only two chairs in the house so decided to sit down on the floor. Svet's wife ushered me to sit back in the chair, but a simple gesture of "It's good to stretch my legs" let me stay where I was. We sat down to some food with little conversation. I was exhausted.

 Shortly after dinner ended, Svet and is wife went to bed. To this day I do not know where they stayed but I was left in the house all by myself. I begged that I wasn't making them forgo their bed. A bowl was left for me to wash and I cleaned myself the best I could. It only took a few passes to turn the water black but I felt whole and made my way to use the outhouse. If you're unfamiliar with an outhouse, it is a structure no bigger than two and a half square feet and about seven feet tall with wooden walls, floor and roof, and a hole cut in the bottom leading to a large pit below. I was careful not to tread too close to the hole while I squatted down and took care of business. I had used something similar on an Indian train whilst travelling the tea plantations and backwaters of Kerala. On the train, there was a big rope handle to anchor yourself from falling backwards. In this outhouse there was little to support yourself and my legs were tired from the day's ride. I could only but laugh as my body shook with its last piece of energy, but it did feel like I completed the business at hand to its fullest. This day was done, on to the next.

The following day came round without realisation that my head had even hit the pillow the night before. The sun had already risen and I had no concept of time. I'd lost track of which day it was a week or so ago and now it was just Day 34 or Day 47. I liked it that way, I was forgetting my world and learning a new one, a world where a moment is everything and nothing. I had no plans so I could focus all of my attention on that moment. Each stranger got my full attention.

I pulled some jeans on and brought myself to the window. Outside was Svet and Tina, he was washing her down with a hose using his thumb over the hole to focus the water - a trick my dad had so often used on his cars and bikes or when he chased my sister and me around the garden on a warm summer's day. My eyes adjusted and as I looked through the small lead lined window I noticed the gear peg had been fixed, the mirror was reattached and the panniers back on. What time was it? How long had Svet been awake?

I scrambled to get on my clothes and rushed outside. Svet raised his head and smiled. He leant back down and continued to wash Tina clean. I signalled to him what he wanted me to do next, but he gently shook his head and moved onto the front wheel. I took a snap on my phone knowing I could never forget this man. What I could learn from him. I thought of myself and how many people I had walked past and not helped, how many of my friends reached out as I was looking the other way.

Svet had fixed my bike and was now refusing any kind of payment. He'd even painted the welds. This was too much, there had to be something. I asked if I could take him, his wife and the English teacher for dinner. He shook his head, once again. Did this guy know any other gesture? I asked Svet if there was anything I could do for the teacher. He said he would ask but first we were to run some errands.

He had a new cardboard box sat in the bed of his truck with an array of brand new motorcycle and car parts, so off we hopped around town delivering the goods. Everyone seemed to wave at Svet. He would always just smile in return, keeping both hands on the wheel. We turned left onto a large road that was well surfaced and pulled up outside of a small hut. I'd seen many of these white huts across Russia. They were Russia's version of the corner shop, selling small loafs of bread that seemed to never age, cigarettes, booze, crisps and chocolate.

Svet hopped out of his truck and signalled 'two' with his fingers and ran inside. I sat there in the passenger seat grateful to have a moment to myself. Behind the white hut was more soviet era housing blocks. As I watched the sky and the clouds drift by a child appeared smoking a cigarette, he must have been all of ten years old. He was dirty and looked guilty. Next to him was an older man that the kid shared his cigarette with. They looked thick as thieves, although not blood-related, you could tell they were close by the way they walked and the little attention they showed one another. I could only imagine what stories they had to share.

The kid approached the truck and stopped a few feet short to finish his cigarette. He was a few drags away from the filter when his face tightened and the colour of his skin drained. He had seen something behind the truck that had scared him. He approached and grabbed onto the bulbar, he moved right to left and back again on the balls of his feet, his eyes honed in on what was happening behind the truck. I tried to use the side mirrors and the rear view mirror to see what he was seeing but with no success. I hadn't heard anything, no screeches of tires or screams but I didn't want to turn my head. He moved near the passenger door, still, not for a second averting his gaze from the thing that was causing him this terror. To my right, I finally saw what he had been looking at.

It was a large set man, with a flat head and short hair, he was clearly drunk and angered. He was waving and beckoning for the child to come over, the other guy that arrived with the kid moved back the way he came and out of sight. Leaving the kid on his own as the stranger approached, his mood swung between anger and upturned palms, trying to show no harm would come, but the kid kept the truck between them. As the drunk got closer I could see his palms were a dark red, dripping red. It was blood, both hands were covered in blood. I, as was the kid, stared at the drunk as he approached, I had no clue on what he would do. My stare was broken when the boy bolted from sight and the drunk stumbled after him. I stayed planted in my seat, heart pounding and watched, as the chase disappeared into the housing estate.

Svet sauntered soon after from the shop and jumped back in the truck. I sat there rooted in silence with a racing heartbeat, not sure what had happened, what to do and definitely not what to say. Svet reversed into the main road and started back the way we came. He was speaking on the phone and I was happy to have the time to calm my nerves. I looked back over my shoulder one last time and hoped the boy was safe. Svet turned down a side road towards his next delivery, Svet ended his call and turned to me, he had spoken to 'Anna the English', which was what Svet referred to her as. Each time he did a smile of mischievous delight came on his face with the pride of speaking another language. How truly privileged I was to speak English, yet utterly lazy towards the other languages I had tried. English helped me out in this global jungle, I just wish I had learnt more. Cantonese, Russian, French, Spanish or any that sounded beautiful to the tongue.

We finally came to rest outside a large cluster of buildings at the end of a lane. It was the local school. It must have been playtime as children were all around. I wondered if Svet and his wife had children. I had not seen any pictures or heard them speak of them. I feel so at home around children, the energy and optimism, the laughs and games and most importantly the imagination, so untainted and free. Back home I would listen to my niece and nephew struggle to spew words at the rate in which their imaginations would work. They would often repeat words as their mouths caught up with their thoughts 'and and and then he said'. I was really happy to be around such energy, and I knew an energy as strong as a child's could easily transcend any language barriers we had.

I knew it would be harder to do the expedition if I had young children at home but I relished in the idea of having my own family one day. What adventures we would go on, what trouble we would cause.

Anna stood at the school gate waiting for us. Svet stayed by the truck and she waved him away, I was unsure of the plan, if any actually existed, but I trusted them. We walked across the large playground.

'Would you mind teaching my class some English phrases, maybe some slang?' she chuckled.

'Sure,' I replied.

'We don't have many travellers come through so this could be a real treat for them,' she added.

'Sure,' I replied.

Surrounded by a throng of kids we walked inside to start my day as an English teacher in far eastern Russia.

We walked in silence as we made our way through the classic school corridors of numbered doors, wooden floors and simple paint. I was shown into the teachers' lounge where I was to wait until class began, but word had got out and the lounge door snapped open. Fifteen or so children filled the door frame with large grins, giggles and malcontent. Anna shooed them back into the corridor and apologised to me, I was smiling and explained it was no trouble, smiling and shaking my head to extenuate my point.

The bell rung yet the children stayed fixed by the door, repeated orders in the soft voice of Anna had them reluctantly walking back to their next class. Anna and I shortly followed and I found myself in front of a class of thirty or so. I scanned the ranks and there sat all the groups that were at my school, the overdeveloped boys with spots and aggression ready to get bent out of shape on the smallest glance, the disappointed girls with 'eww, he's gross' scrolled across the down turned lips and frown lines. There was the needy kid desperate for love and attention that sat with neatly brushed hair and the look of 'ask me the question else I'll pop' on his face and the kid avoiding eye contact at all costs just in case the world implodes. I wondered where I was sat, the fat ginger kid waiting for his growth spurt to start and puberty to kick in.

'How are you?' I asked.

Anna waved her hands like a conductor at the kids.

'We are well, thank you,' they retorted.

'What phrases do you all know?' I enquired.

'How are you?' Needy squealed.

'What time is it?' Another added.

'Where is the train station?'

'How much is the apple?'

The disappointed girls stayed silent and the thirteen going on forty kickboxer stared venomously looking for any excuse to march to the front of the class and sock me one.

'These are all great questions,' I said. 'Let's start a conversation,' I continued, looking to Anna for reassurance, she looked more worried than the doomsday kid.

'Their English is little,' she said.

'What footballs teams do you know?'

'Manchester United.'

'Chelsea.'

'Do you know where Chelsea football stadium is?'

I panicked, I hadn't a clue, I knew it was in London, but where in London? I had no interest in football, rugby was my Dad's game. I liked climbing, surfing and bikes. They could say what they wanted, I'd just agree, sounds like a solid plan. Misinformation to avoid misrepresentation, maybe I should go into politics?

'It's in London,' a kid at the back blurted.

'Well done,' I said.

I turned to one of the girls. 'How are you?'

'I am fine, thank you,' she replied, looking to Anna for confirmation.

'What is your favourite subject at school?' I continued.

She looked petrified, staring at Anna. Anna asked her the question in Russian.

'Science.' the girl responded.

We went back and forth from class to class for the remainder of the day. I got all of Anna's class together for a large team photo and I was on my way. It had been so much fun teaching the kids English, watching them go from fear to full on enthusiasm was a wonderful sight. I sat by the school wall waiting for Svet to return, tapping my heels against the stone wall. I knew immediately this would be one of the best stories of the trip, a lesson of greatness for me, and friends to always remember. I knew I'd probably never speak with any of them again but I'd hold them close.

That night Svet had friends coming for dinner and we had to pick some meat for the pot. I asked Svet if there was a bath or shower in town that I could go to, to get clean. Although I had washed in the bowl, the majority of my body was still covered in the dirt and crime of the last few days, I made sure to emphasize on a public shower, as it seemed an item of high privilege to have running hot water at home and I was careful that I didn't offend. That night I was taken to Svet's wife's sister that lived in one of the soviet era blocks and had a running shower. Svet and his sister-in-law sat in the lounge whilst I quickly washed myself, conscious not to waste water, even though I was craving to stand in the hot steam and water for several days. Another bizarre and truly beautiful gift from a family I'd only met 48 hours prior.

Tina was fixed, I had paid my dues and Svet had to get back to work, time to move on. I was eager for the road or maybe it was calling me, either way I had no choice but to obey.

I rode to the outskirts of town as Svet skipped and skimmed easily across the pothole-ridden streets. One day I would find his ease behind the grips but for now, I was deeply proud and thankful to be riding with him. This was his land, like a bear that strolls confidently in the woods, Svet was truly free on his bike. We road up the fresh tarmac that I should have taken to get into town, and I was back on the Trans-Siberian Highway.

Svet's orange KTM stopped, he kicked out the stand and walked over to me, he hugged me deeply catching me by surprise, another sign of heart from this land. I felt ashamed of the times when people needed that kind of love from me, but I chose to look the other way, towards things that I said were more important but in truth just offered an escape from me taking ownership. Sophie, my ex-girlfriend, was a beautifully talented artist and designer. She rose quickly with some prominent brands in London and was on the cusp of starting her own show, yet my failed business and a longing to be anywhere but London kept her at arm's length. When she wanted to move things forward I regressed, she deserved the honesty that my heart wasn't in it but all I did was say enough to keep her by my side without making any real progress. I had always thought of myself as a caring a person, maybe I was just selfish.

I was so thankful for taking that wrong turn, otherwise, I'd never had got to know this place the way I know it now. As a deep heart behind dirty hands. Like trying to hold a marlin on a line with your bare hands, I was forced to let go. It freed me to think of the good times ahead, on this trip and at home with Libby.

I had been told to stay away from sleeping rough along the highway as many bandits lurked and preyed. During the last five years, people had disappeared and others murdered. I didn't know if this was sensationalism, usually instigated by people that had not been far from their own front door or the actual truth. The vivid images of the taxi driver exchanging insurance details with the biker and the terrified kid in Svobodny made me extremely cautious, so I agreed to ride the nine hundred kilometres to the next town in one day.

The day was, as expected exceptionally long yet passed by with little struggle, the road condition stayed a constant shabby grit which allowed me to cruise easily. Around midday I hit another stretch of one hundred and fifty kilometres of pure tarmac. Later, when I was in Chita, they explained the road was so good because it ran by the hometown of a finance minister, now in Moscow; distribution of wealth at its best.

Tonight's place of rest sat on the great intersection of the Trans-Siberian highway and the road to Tynda and, ultimately, Magadan. It was still very early in the year and there was a large probability that the road I aimed to take from Tynda to the northern tip of lake Baikal would not be open because the melt water would be running too high for me to cross. I hoped tonight I would be able to find out.

I was staying with another friend of a friend of a friend, and this time, I was too tired to learn any great truths so I made sure I found the right turning into town. At the entrance of Skovorodino sat my host, a true biker in the most literal sense of the American word, a ponytail, a leather waistcoat, a belly, a Harley and tats. My first thought was what did this guy do? Here we were in the middle of Siberia and this guy was on the latest Harley with the white walled tires, saddle bags and open throat exhaust. I pulled in behind him and unplugged from the bike.

'Good ride?' he asked.

'Pretty straight forward,' I concluded.

'We go to the Motorcycle Club, my friends want to meet you,' he continued.

I hopped back on Tina and followed him into town, I was exhausted, today had been my longest ride and I'd only stopped for fuel, I hadn't really eaten. I would get into a state where my body would stop, I never fatigued, the sky did not move nor did I hunger for a meal until the day was done then it thumped me in the back, hard and deep. I knew I was to be thankful for the hospitality but tonight I wanted to sleep, I would be happy next to Tina on a patch of fresh grass, she was all I needed, but I had found myself behind another Soviet housing block in front of more concrete garages.

We pulled to rest next to an already open garage, inside was a leather couch, a fridge and a flag of what must have been their chapter. I walked inside, looking around, thinking this would be perfect for me to lay my head for the night. As I pushed the couch with my hand, I heard a bike start, I wheeled round and saw Viktor riding off. I hadn't a clue where he was going, so there I stood in the garage with Tina on my own. I sat down on the ground and stretched my legs, being my height on Tina was pretty snug.

The sun was setting behind the town and I was struggling to keep my eyes open, about forty minutes passed as I sat questioning the outcome of tonight, was it murder, party or rest? I hoped it was the last of the options but who knows, this could have been the devil's bed, all I knew is that anything could happen.

Another hour passed and the sun had fully set when a car pulled down the alley. The headlights made it hard to see who was inside, I pressed my back against the wall. The driver was my height yet half my weight, he wore thick yellowed glasses and a grey shirt under an old cardigan. His trousers were way too big for him, held to his dilapidated hips with an old brown belt, on his feet he wore open sandals and socks. His face was yellow and withdrawn, with a large hook nose that protruded out from his face seemingly holding his skull together. Thin hair wisped over his head as a yellowed mouth drew on a cigarette, he was enough to put the hardiest of offenders on edge. Viktor was in the passenger seat and the two in the rear personified the classic brick shit houses. No one spoke as they got out the car, Viktor put his arm around my shoulders, pulling me down to his height.

'We have a hotel for you to stay, your bike is safe here, we go to the hotel.'

'I'm fine sleeping here,' I remarked. I had everything on the bike and I did not feel relaxed with these guys.

'No no, good hotel, nice bed,' Viktor pushed.

I had little choice. I grabbed what little I could and piled into the car, I'm not sure if it was me, but the car stunk. Something had died in here, hopefully, I wasn't to be the second. I sat between the two giants in the back, with their shot-put shoulders and my padded motorcycle jacket we were like peas in a pod, albeit giant leather-cloaked, skinhead peas. I was hungry, if I could get settled into this apparent "hotel" then I could go out for a walk and find some noodles or something simple. The idea of food became an inventive tool to help alleviate the fear of being murdered. Although I did wonder how they'd do it? In my current position all they'd need to do was take a simultaneous deep breath and I'd pop like a grape. That image, the idea of my inners spraying the inside of the car, covering every window and face made me chuckle. I was tired.

We drove for all of five minutes and pulled to rest outside a large soviet housing block, just like all the other ones I had seen since leaving Vladivostok. Many windows were blocked with wood and numerous others had nothing but the darkness inside, the ground at the foot of this building was nothing but dirt, heavily potted by winter and tires.

'You stay here, fifty dollars,' Viktor explained.

'Where? Here?' I pointed.

'Yes, good shower, good bed.' Viktor nodded.

'Oh, I am staying with you?'

Maybe Viktor had changed his mind

'No, this hotel.'

'It's OK, I'll stay with my bike. Tomorrow I leave early.'

'What time do you want to go?' Viktor asked.

'Six?'

'Ok, six is fine, you go six, now hotel.'

I didn't want to push much harder, I felt on edge, off balanced, ready for my luck to run out.

We walked into the building, the front door was a large steel door with heavy bolts on the outside. Do they lock you in at night? I wanted to trust them, I truly did but my instincts said otherwise, deep down in the depths, maybe it was how cold Viktor was acting or the hysterically clichéd crew of sex offenders and henchmen that were with him.

We marched up six flights of stairs, each flight had eight steps, forty-eight in total, plus another three steps to the front door. I counted my route because the stairwell was pitch black, Viktor carried a light, shining the steps as we walked, until he stopped and raised the torch to a door, just as heavy and industrial as the front door. Viktor ruffled through a large set of keys held on a metal circle. He opened the door to present another, this one looked like a normal front door, with a letter box, opaque glass and red paint. This door was open and we all piled in.

There were family pictures on the wall, ornaments everywhere, someone's laundry sat in a basket by the bed, the bed sat in the main room along with a garden set of table and chairs, next door was a small kitchen and a further door, which I hoped to be the bathroom.

'Are you hungry?' Viktor asked.

'Yes, very.' I smiled.

He left again taking his sidekicks with him. I went from scared to confused, whose apartment was this? Where were the occupants? Where had Viktor gone? Did he kick someone out for me? I hope not. I needed to sleep, I was exhausted. I was cold. I walked to the front doors and locked both of them. I must stay awake, where was Viktor?

I sat down in the kitchen, if I were to get close to that bed that would be it. Unconscious bliss. I heard the locks turn, Viktor was back, but there was a commotion, the door flung open to Viktor and his crew, and now seven others, they all carried alcohol and one had a boom box. I wanted noodles and sleep, it looked like that was going to have to wait.

The boom box was pushed onto the kitchen table and out came death metal, hardcore, screaming, death metal, seemingly at one volume, maximum. I've heard of people committing group suicides to this type of music, maybe we could try that, at least I'd get a nap and I'd stop craving noodles.

Vodka came flowing my way, but this time I had no way to deflect, after the first three I was close to being sick. Of the members that had joined solely for this party, three were already trashed, a short fat man that grinned profusely at me, took a perch on my lap and muttered away in Russian. If this group suicide wasn't going to happen I needed another strategy. I pushed Grinner off my lap and he stumbled back towards the Vodka, still muttering as he went. Viktor was now smiling, it all came into place, he wanted to show off, he wanted to rage and party with the westerner, unfortunately, this westerner had been averaging seven hundred kilometres a day.

After comparing notes on the beauty of death metal, I bent my arm onto the waxed canvas table cloth and rested my head, adrenaline was surging and I could feel the tiredness going away, but tomorrow was another nine hundred kilometre day. I flitted between resting my head to trying to converse. The Vodka kicked in and the room started to spin, I hadn't eaten since breakfast. I rested my head again, I really needed food or I was going to be sick. Ever since I had passed out on my hometown police station steps at the age of 17 due to partying a little too hard, the mere smell of Vodka made me heave. Viktor noticed me sleeping on the table and stopped the music, just as quick as all his actions, they were leaving. I felt bad, they were showing me their kind of a good time, but I had to listen to my body. We agreed to meet outside at 6 a.m. and I locked the doors behind them.

The bed caught me as I fell backwards, the room was spinning and I was trying hard for it to stop. I forced two fingers down my throat in an attempt to rid my body of any more that was sat unconsumed, nothing but bile came up. I found my way to the kitchen and began to raid the cupboards, they were bare. Tiredness won the battle.

I awoke at 5 a.m., I had stopped needing an alarm some time ago. When you have a purpose as grand as this, nothing stops the body. I got dressed and found my way down the black stairs to see Viktor waiting in the car for me outside, I was tired, hungry and hungover. Through all the chaos I had forgotten to ask Viktor about the track to the northern tip of lake Baikal, known as the BAM. I had the Trans-Siberian route and the BAM already plotted in. I showed Viktor the BAM and he started laughing.

'Much water, no trucks yet, too early in the season.'

'How long until the logging trucks start?'

'Two months.'

With my hangover, I put up little fight to the fact I wouldn't tackle the BAM, so Tina and me continued on the Tran-Siberian.

Tina was running so smooth, she never grumbled or complained, never mocked the fuel from the various sources I took her too, she just kept going. She was small and petite now, a little red and white tank on top of a simple frame and a beautiful sounding engine. I hadn't even had a puncture, the bags were secure and the music blasted.

I had only covered twenty miles when I saw a rest stop, with the bike full I proceeded to stuff my face with a variety of processed food desperate to instill my body with the energy needed for the day ahead.

I was nearing Mongolia, the mystery of the trip. It was mystical, spiritual, rugged and bare. Adventure books existed because Mongolia did, it was up there with Tibet, Himalayas and the Arctic.

The road trucked on just as it had for the thousands of miles that sat behind me. Traces of a recent forest fire started to appear to the north, it became a game of much amusement as the burnt stumps passed my periphery at speed, creating wonderful images. I saw dolphins diving, panthers on their hind legs, contorted figures and shooting stars.

Time itself seemed to disappear, it hadn't slowed, but just left me altogether. Time was a being and he had walked away to pursue someone else. The miles had been ticking down at a steady pace and I was in the groove, there was a sweet smell in the air with the morning trees and I disappeared into a daze.

Locked inside this helmet for twelve hours a day, took my mind to wonderful depths. My mind was detaching; I did not worry about my body as he continued under his own devices on the bike. He filled Tina with fuel when necessary and gave his organs the needed energy and water and kept on moving. My mind left the conscious state, I flitted between the trees as I flew along next to my body, I was not cold nor hot, tired or awake.

From the trees I swung, I was now back in South Africa looking at my first girlfriend, she was married now and with children. My heart was shattered when we ended, it took me almost two years to get over her, to move to the point where she was nothing more than a memory. Then I swung again, like an ape on a vine. I was with Sophie, seven years of my life and we walked away and hadn't spoken a word since. Should I seek closure, should I write her an apology letter?

I didn't believe I was a bad person but I knew I had made it hard. I was hard on myself, I was conflicted in London, I didn't belong there. The city drained me so I was hard on her, spiteful and brash, cowardly and untrue. We hadn't loved one another for years but comfort kept us together. She'd met a rugby player in the north of England and moved to be with him. It happened fast, she must have been seeing him prior to us parting ways. I didn't blame her as I had put her there, I could clearly see that now. What a brute I was, the night she said goodbye I drank half a bottle of scotch, hoping to burn the spinning into something less harmful, I flitted between angry and desolation. I hit myself, heavy thumping blows to my temple, what a fucking idiot I'd been. I had sworn I was right and now it was clear I was wrong, wrong in my actions. I didn't know how to hold myself when I cared for someone so much and completed the polar opposite of what was needed, the need for compassion, humility, vulnerability and honest love.

The night we split up, sleep kept away, so I ran the streets, bruised and drunk. I clattered into cars and walls. I vomited over someone's wall into their garden, the cold air hitting the back of my throat bringing me into reality. I'd looked around heavily dazed and confused. I had nothing on my feet, just a pair of jeans and no top. I hadn't been angry that we split but I was terrified of what I'd done, to someone so sweet and graceful.

Now I was here, with Tina riding along with the earth spinning under my feet and all I could think of were my wrongs. they consumed me, the tears rolled, these thoughts took every ounce of energy I had left. I cried until I could not cry anymore and then I said sorry to myself. My chest opened and I said sorry again, I knew if I relived those selfish actions I would be on my own again. I agreed with myself I was a good man with a good heart and it was okay to let this go, the road ahead was what mattered.

Then I thought of Libby, I knew I would get better, I'd calm. I just hoped that I held true. I wanted to be oak for her, a shield and an arm, a laugh, a smile and a compassionate ear. I hoped so, I know I will, I will work at it nonstop, like my mother said, "If you want marriage to work then work hard." Looking back, it was probably more for self-reassurance than guidance to me and my sister. I knew I could work hard, I knew I wasn't the fastest or strongest or smartest but I'd outwork anyone and I'd have the prize, Libby by my side. I smiled and let go further, a red hot temper surged through my veins, of passion and strength, everything I would give to Libby.

Flashes of frowning sad faces now filled the horizon, thoughts of the way I had spoken to people in the past echoed in my head. The wrongs I could never right, like a ship too heavy on a weak sea. I would work it all out. I circled back around my body like a summer cloud over a mountain top gently rising on the air. It turned my heart inside out and I apologised to them as well, again I agreed with myself I wasn't a bad guy just a lot to learn. Shit, I thought I knew it all at eighteen after visiting South Africa and Borneo, then again at twenty-four. Looking back, I knew nothing at eighteen or twenty-four or now at twenty-eight.

On we went... I swam with the burnt trees, running my fingers in the charcoal as I flew, my hands were black, deep deep black. I painted the clouds as I watched myself riding to my left, I was one of the Lost Boys and there was Peter, sat merged with a motorcycle, roaring down the road. I swam back and sat on my shoulder, just enjoying the world. I said sorry to everyone, I said sorry to Libby for my future wrongs, as the wind pushed in a new. The road ahead ran straight to the horizon, but I knew the secret, another horizon was waiting for me when I got there, and the one after that, as it would all the way home on this marble drifting violently in endless space. My tears had stopped and I was feeling lighter than I ever had, I could breathe, I had a third lung and oxygen poured in.

Still sat on my shoulder I looked out to my right, in amongst the trees was a bear, not the Asiatic black bear I had read so much about but a Turquoise blue bear sat on his bum looking at me. He sat beside a log under an old Birch, his belly resting gently on his outstretched hind legs with his front legs by his side and his paws turn skyward. His fur was thick and warm and clumped together around a large wet nose. His eyes were big, broad and deep, they knew something I couldn't comprehend. Was this bear here for me? If so, why did I deserve this bear? Why had he come to see me?

He stayed planted on his bottom as his deep brown eyes followed me along the horizon. I lost sight of him as I rode round a bend, only to have him appear in front of me, hovering, silently in the air, he was graceful enough to avoid disturbing the sound of the wind through the leaves and the scent of spruce and pine.

We were seemingly indifferent, I was losing my mind, I had lost my mind. I couldn't continue like this, my days were numbered, I was to be sanctioned and thrown away, 'a pathetic attempt at a grand adventure' the headline would read. He wasn't talking to me but I knew he was a he, not a she or nothing at all. He had been here since the dawn of time and held keys to untold wisdom. We held a strong connection, like a hand or foot or childhood memory, something that was yours and yours alone. I should stop and ask a couple of questions. I failed to push the matter and we just kept on, with a heavy face, I didn't know what I would ask him.

Eternity soon passed and then I could see the answer to why he was here, he was me, and this world, and I was him. I had forgotten the motorcycle and simply gazed, benign and irreverent to what was in front of me. I was in a state of eternal bliss. I had let myself off for the wrongs I had done and made an agreement with myself in times to come to hold true on being the man that Libby deserved. I was in a lifting bliss, nothing in this world could touch me.

With a flash, the front wheel dropped hard. I had hit a pothole. I opened my eyes with a start. Had I been asleep? I braked hard pulling the bike to the side of the road, I yanked my headphones through my helmet and took my helmet off, fumbling with the chin strap, my heart was pounding and my diaphragm drew long hard clumps of oxygen deep into my body. I focused down on my breathing to settle myself. Holy shit, I had fallen asleep.

Looking around the road, it was clear and empty. I sighed and acknowledged my stupid luck. I questioned myself what had happened. I had dozed off behind the bars, for how long I don't know. I couldn't remember my eyes closing. Last night's antics were taking its toll and I had done the one thing I swore I would not do, I'd pushed myself too far, the combination of the offered hospitality, bandits and crashes. I had bitten too deep into the adventure. I wasn't here to win the race but explore the world on the back of a motorcycle. Why was I cranking out these huge miles?

Stupid, foolhardy and recklessly myopic. I was exhausted, cold and tired. I craved for Libby or an empty iceberg, floating majestically out in the deep black water, a place where I could rest and forget who I was. To have a shower, a deep sleep and some vegetables, holy fuck I needed some vegetables, peas or brittle carrots. I wanted a kiss and a pillow. I dreamed of laying my heart to rest, being free, for the simple pleasure of breathing out, and at the end of that breath, there would be nothing. A deep long black sleep for me to spiral into and complete my story, my time on earth and simply rest. I was cold. I got off the bike and sat with my back on the engine case, I hovered a gaze out into the trees hoping to see the blue bear again. He never came and I drifted into a deep sleep next to Tina on the side of the road.

Later that day I finally arrived in Ulan Ude, the last stop before Mongolia. In the planning process, I found it was easier to get my Mongolian Visa in Ulan Ude than in Boston. I had scheduled three days to get my Visa, see the city, get some supplies and hit the road to Ulaanbaatar.

My visa was easier than I expected, I completed the forms and would come back the following day to get my passport. The city held little to keep my attention other than a large bust of Stalin sat in the middle of town. I rested well in a basic hotel and fed my fill on noodles and fruit. Tina was packed, fuelled and ready to go. I planned on changing my road tires to the TKCs in Mongolia, ready for the desert and the backcountry.

I was lucky to stumble on a coffee shop with decent Wi-Fi so I spent the time updating relatives and talking to Libby. The city held little in the way of attractions and frankly I was bored of statues, so I took the time to rest. I reread Jupiter Travels for the umpteenth time feeling somehow related to Ted Simon, now I was here, so far from normality, home and my family. All his words took on a new meaning giving me a great release of pent up anxiety and stress that had been building. After a few more packs of noodles, borscht and some unknown but very delightful sweet it was time for me to move on.

My road tires came to bite me on the last few miles of Russia before I hit the Mongolian border, when I hit deep sand the bike pinged me over the bars once again, this time, a truck was tailgating me and came to a stop close to my head. He shook his head, drove around and trundled on. A calmness came over me compared to how I felt in Svobodny - it was night and day. I casually raised the bike, strapped the broken panniers to the bike with some spare straps, bent the foot brake into shape and started the bike and rode on. Nothing was going to stop me.

Mongolia is four times the size of the UK and only ten percent paved road in a network of fifty thousand kilometres. I was nervous, excited and eager to get to Ulan Bator. I had made it through Siberia, whilst I hadn't taken the BAM, which was *the* overland adventure route, the Trans-Siberian highway had been epic, with such overwhelming experiences, such beautiful and fearsome people. The stoic behaviour imbued on a landscape driven by political ideals that left it like a twentieth century wild west.

I pulled to rest at the Mongolian border. I took my helmet off and savoured the moment. Tina and I were here, we had crossed America and Canada, South Korea and Siberia. I was so deeply content, a deep geophysical force spinning like a centrifuge in me, pulling me in tight to the earth, where nothing could knock me over.

Preparing Tina in my apartment in Boston.

My Boston 'garage'.

Tina complete and ready to go.

Day 1. Boston. Hot, sweaty and extremely nervous.

One of the many family members that looked after me whilst going across North America.

An evening ride in Texas.

First problem of the ride. An oil leak in Utah.

Enjoying the Rockies.

Tina making friends on the ferry.

Deception Pass. Just before the Canadian border.

Living the hard life in Vancouver. Flying around the islands whilst I waited for my bike to be shipped to Seoul, South Korea.

Enjoying the delights of South Korea.

Sergey and Tina, en route to Khabarovsk, Russia.

Let the Russian fun begin.

Being interviewed for Russian TV

Getting in the groove on the Trans-Siberian Highway.

My day teaching English in Svobodny.

Lenin.

First few miles in Mongolia.

Chasing down the fuel trucks.

Stoic children of Ulaanbaatar, Mongolia.

The truck that picked me up after the frame broke.

Last and best days' ride in Mongolia.

The Altai, Russia.

Having fun in Kazakhstan in the 110 Degree heat.

Sedlec Ossuary, Czech Republic.

Waiting in Calais, France.

26,000kms. I had done it!

MONGOLIA

The border was over quickly as Tina and I rode for fifty miles before I had to pull over, I had to soak it all in. This was surreal. The road was beautifully smooth, raised above the plateau as far the eye could see. As I headed south, the east disappeared to shallow hills and the sky. To the west, the grasses ran far to the mountains that rose on a distant horizon.

My first camel came into a view a few miles in, this shaggy beast was losing its winter coat and stood to feed on the abundant grass. I stopped Tina again and took some pictures. The sky was beautifully blue, warming my back as I walked out away from the road towards the camels, hidden behind a rock was half of a camel down on its side, a camel carcass. This was the only evidence of wolves I would see during my trip but their impact was viciously real. I had been warned about the dogs the herders kept to protect their flocks against the packs. They were far more dangerous than the wolves, as they had little fear of man and would readily chase a man on a bike. The carcass was fresh with little of the bone and coat or flesh remaining. The head and neck remained intact and I hoped the wolves weren't nearby ready to finish their supper. Maybe the necks of camels were like the trunks of Elephants and were left by predators.

I followed the road down to Ulan Bator in utter bliss, the drummers were drumming, the choir was deep and harmonising, I was truly free. Ulan Bator was a plethora of half-built houses, rubble, one story boxes, yurts, office buildings, hotels, bars, and individual shops. The streets were filthy, dust, sand and dirt flew heavily in the air, packed cars gave no regard to this man on a bike. I ducked and dived through the traffic, giving regular slaps on car bonnets of over-eager commuters. Tina roared, in a low gear with a quick snap of throttle she barked beautifully, a sound I had cherished but doubted if anyone held my glee.

My satnav easily made its way to the Oasis Motel, this was Ulan Bator's mecca for overlanders run by a dutch lady called Sybille. I was excited to speak with some fluent English bodies and enjoy the European breakfasts. I couldn't remember a time when I had craved processed meats and hard boiled eggs any more. The hostel sign hung out over the heavily potted road, a large metal gate hid the parking at the back of the hostel. I opened the throttle and the gate rolled back, the yard held about four yurts, decking and space for bikes. There were two BMWs and a Tenere, it was Dutch's. I pulled in next to Dutch's bike and kicked out the side stand. I needed a foot to spread the weight of the stand so I used a large stone, watching the stand for twenty seconds, she held firm. I left everything on the bike as I made my way inside to find out who was around.

'Holy shit,' I blurted out loud to the empty room. They had Toblerone. I knew I was going to have fun.

Sybille circled around the corner and entered the room with what I would learn to be her trademark grin. She stood all of five feet tall, with short blonde hair cut neatly at the jaw, extenuating her chubby rosy cheeks, framing a puckered smile. I always wonder how people end up in the places they do, why was this petite little Dutch lady half way around the world running a hostel? She welcomed me and explained the setup and rooms available. I agreed to have one of the bunk beds in the dorm rooms as the beds were bigger than those in the yurts and I looked forward to some days resting and being off the bike. I had been on the road for a little over seven weeks and I'd been moving at a fair pace. Rest is so much richer when you earn it.

No one else seemed to be around so I squared my belongings away under my bunk. Along the window sill I placed the key essentials of a headtorch and toilet paper, also known as TP, so they were close at hand. On came the trusty jeans and the oily t-shirt and I made my way back down to the mess to order some lunch. Whilst my sandwich was being made I was shown round the showers, these were shared showers for the neighbourhood. Many buildings didn't have the luxury of running water and many Mongolians still lived in Yurts, albeit permanently rooted within their capital city.

The sharing economy extended beyond showers, to tools and appliances and most prominently hitching a ride. All you had to do was wave by the side of the road and someone would stop and offer a ride to where you needed to go for a small fee, as long as it was along or nearby the route they were heading. I couldn't imagine it back home, where mistrust is usually the first reaction.

Attached to the showers was a small hairdresser that was full of people chatting with little to no cutting actually happening. They smiled contently as I poked my head into the doorway, then turned and continued their conversation. I ate my lunch and hung around the beams of sunshine dancing across the city. Dutch was apparently out running errands, so I headed up to my dormitory and fell into a gentle dream.

Dutch soon returned, ploughing heavily into the dorm room, carrying bags and boxes making an awful racket, waking me with a start. The sun was strong and had warmed me to boiling while I had laid asleep. It took him only seconds to recognise me and in a sweaty daze, I gave the balding Dutch man one long hug. He'd arrived only a day earlier and had come via another border riding quite away across rough terrain that had taken a toll on him and his bike. He had also planned to stay in Ulan Bator for around a week, resting and preparing his bike for the next leg of the trip. My whole trip was planned to last three months, Dutch had already been on the road for three years and had another year left riding before returning home to his father's house on the outskirts of Amsterdam.

Dutch was in his late thirties and had decided to give up his career as an electrician in the local town. He sold his house and a majority of his belongings and set off, not looking back on his epic adventure. I listened vividly to the stories of South America and the run-ins he had with dogs and cartels, bushwhacking through thick brush and riding nearly a thousand miles down the wrong track only to turn around. The conversation continued out to his bike, where he showed me her scars, crude filler covering gashes in the plastic tank and all but one of his indicators were held on with tape. We discussed our routes across Mongolia. I had planned to head south on the more heavily travelled route along the Gobi, Dutch was toying with the idea of running the central route which offered more challenge and time by himself. He had been told to stay away from the northern route as the melt water was high and the wetland was yet to dry to a manageable point.

Dutch and I stood bare foot in the parking lot as I gave him a tour of Tina and her upgrades, from the Ohlin's shocks on the rear, the rebuilt front forks that held sealed gas cylinders, down to the sealed spoked wheels that allowed me to run both tubeless and tubed tires depending on the terrain. The metal mule panniers looked huge compared to Dutch's, who had opted for soft luggage, he rode compact and light and purposeful. Tina in comparison looked like a travelling gipsy, with trinkets and bangles hanging merrily from every edge. Dutch was amazed I had got here on the tires I had, only to explain of my foibles en route. Even with the TKCs crossing Mongolia was going to be tough on this bike he concluded. The weight alone was huge compared to his combined with relatively very little power. I couldn't do much else than shrug my shoulders and make my way back inside.

Dutch was going to head east for a week or so to see a famous statue then head back to Ulan before continuing west. I had planned for five days in Ulan Bator and asked Dutch on what I should see. He responded, 'Not much, it's pretty boring around here, although you should check out the black market.' I smiled and sat down at one of the dinner tables as he headed upstairs.

The evening drew round and with the night bringing in cool air from the north. Slowly the hostel filled up with locals helping Sybille and a few residents that had been here a while. The most notable were two Korean girls working at a nearby school for the summer to improve their English; Demetri, a Frenchman who moved to Washington state in his early twenties and had stayed there working for a small company at the time called Microsoft. With his "golden parachute" as he called it, retired early and set out to circumnavigate the globe solely by human power. He would row the oceans, ski the snow and ice and cycle the rest. He had crossed the Bering Strait last winter and had finally made his way down to Mongolia via a ninety-day stint in jail in northern Siberia due to paperwork confusion. He wore his hair long and nature had made it grey. He looked surprisingly out of shape for someone completing such a feat, a point in which he soon rectified by advising he needed the energy stores for the big hundred miles a day he tried to complete across Russia and Mongolia and eventually down into the 'Stan's.

I went for a shower and for the first time since leaving North America, would be able to video call Libby back home, the hostel had fast Wi-Fi and I was beyond ecstatic to see her gorgeous face. I sat down in the shower cubicle on a slatted wooden bench and waited for the connection to make the assuring 'bring bring'. My phone stopped ringing and a connection was made, the video seemed to take forever to illuminate her face. Suddenly she took the screen, overwhelmed with things to say to one another we sat there in silence grinning hopelessly for a good few minutes until she reeled out in her warming voice, 'How are you doing?' All of the stories I could tell her competed with one another for the forefront of my mind with none of them winning decisively, leading to a short and brief chat about the hostel and things back home in Boston. I cut the call short by saying the shower was needed by someone else, we kissed the camera and said our goodbyes.

It had hit me like a sledgehammer, I was massively homesick, homesick for a house on the east coast of a foreign country. They say home is where the heart is and I knew then it would simply be wherever Libby was. I dropped my head and began to cry, it was short lived as the heat of the shower soon soothed my fears away and turned my thoughts to her smile, her body and little things I'll never mention, leaving me content and tired.

Demetri, the two Koreans and I sat down and ate dinner together, I dived deeply into my plate of schnitzel and mashed potatoes, enjoying every mouthful. The Koreans had brought their English books to the table, to prepare for the following day. Demetri had noticed their text books made little in the way of confidence for the author as the cover page wrote the title 'Basic Engilsh'. The absurdity of this simple typo sent me into hysterics, the kind that hurt your cheeks and sides, the kind that people shuffle slowly away from you as you snort and wheeze with your final breaths. It was like a water main had been let off and I allowed all this emotion to charge readily through my body. Again, another sign I was relaxing into my world around me, letting the journey take me, instead of this stiff upper lip approach I had taken, under some misconceived notion of survival that was required to complete such an adventure.

One of the Korean girls and I settled in with a beer to listen to more of Demetri's stories and his planned assault on such a huge expedition. During periods where winter was needed in order to progress, he simply travelled as far as he could until the seasons started to change then would head home and await the winter to resume again. This luxury he had afforded himself gave him the time to soak in the world around him, combined with the average speed of hauling on skis, he had grown to have an intimate knowledge of the people and wilderness that was around him. He had now reversed the process and travelled only during the spring and summer months whilst on his bike, he was working on getting his wife a visa so she could join him on the memorable legs.

Mongolia was the most sparsely populated country in the world, with their guttural singing monks hidden in temples and the days gone but not forgotten of the mighty Genghis Khan charging across the great steppe. As a kid, I was mesmerised by the stories of Mongolia, the hunters that use eagles, and the street children who had their own dedicated section in the main newspaper to the deaths that occurred on a daily basis. Demetri said the main cause was falling rubble from badly constructed buildings. Mongolians until very recently led a nomadic lifestyle, but as big business moved in, in the form of oil and natural gas conglomerates the city grew, luring people in with sparkle of high western earnings and a 'better life'.

This promised life rarely materialised leaving waves of people with nothing and those that suffered the most, whether abandoned or left orphaned were these hardy children littering the streets. Stories circulated of the communities that lived in the sewers, down by the hot water pipes, areas they would occupy in order to survive the brutal winters. I only had the fortune of meeting a few of these street kids during my stay but what was abundantly clear was the strength in their eyes on the hardships they faced. It seemed selfish to show tears for their suffering, their faces screamed 'show me no pity, just give me the keys, give me the keys to having my own life beyond the sewers of Ulan Bator'.

The black market sat along one of the main southern roads a few miles or so from Oasis. I had decided to hitch a lift but soon ended the journey short as the traffic seemed to move nowhere. I paid my driver and headed out on foot, I walked with many rough looking kids in tattered clothes and broken shoes. Some went without and stood barefoot, seemingly unaware of the sharp rocks that made the up the ditch.

Just before the black market was the tire market, a vast sea of shipping containers sprawled out across the dust holding every part and mod one could hope for to jazz up their Lada or scooter. I meandered through the containers until I walked into a line of snooker tables, full-size snooker tables lined up, with men drawing heavily on strong cigarettes as the old chipped balls plodded wearily across the torn tables.

Beyond the snooker tables sat more containers that were now selling all you needed to build a yurt, the decoration of the various poles and frames was not that different from canal barges of England, with delicate pin striping and ornate flowers painted on the window frames and doors, just with British green replaced by a deep orange. Heavily lined faces of men and women adorned each container watching me as I passed through. They stayed rooted in their position, propped up against the door or on a small stool, their face and gaze barely changing as my strange face came into their periphery.

Each morning they would come, position their hands on the locks and gently pull back the bolts on the doors of the container, moving back they would allow the large heavy doors to swing open coming to a rest on the container side, then would be their routine of dismantling the intricate packing they had completed the previous night in order to safely store all of their worldly belongings. Strong winters would come and their hands would age but still they would come and dismantle. In front of the container all of the struts, beams, canvases, windows, doors, pegs and nails required to build a beautiful yurt would be laid out for display. Once neatly and safely displayed they would retreat to their perch that would protect them from the sun, the wind, the rain and the snow. Gently they would rub their tired hands, warming the joints as the hours passed waiting for the one family to show and declare that 'I need a new home'. With the purchase a void would be created in their cave of belongings. In time the void would be filled by a cousin, uncle or a father who, with skillful hands along with wood and chisel, plane and craft, would create with accurate ease all of the struts, beams, canvases, windows, doors, pegs and nails required to build a beautiful yurt.

    The black market finally came into view with various stalls made of crude metal legs and chipboard, crammed next to one another, with an intricate and interdependent canopy of tarp and clips. Each stall was the finest purveyor of its own goods, whether that be wolf feet that had been made into a riding whip, Communist Chinese sewing machines or beautiful ornate gypsy saddles for one of the tiny Mongolian horses that outnumbered Mongolians two to one. Stalls were full of brass, copper and greening metal objects, trinkets and boxes and decorative knives as far as the eye could see. Further on came the racks of Mongolian riding boots made from beautifully stitched colourful fabric, with the toes turned up and the lining made of felt helping the wearer overcome the brutal winters. There were rows of Dels, the traditional nomadic coat of the Mongolian, with beautiful geometric shapes intricately woven into the fabric. Beyond the clothes came the furs and pelts and hides of the various animals, from wolves to alpacas, many riders bought the alpaca fur for a cover for their seat, allowing the beauty of thousands of years of evolution to wick the sweat and hold the heat. Every other part of the animal was also for sale in various forms, whether it be stuffed or skinned. I was close to buying a pair of large industrial leather boots that resembled the British wellington boot for a true shit kicker feel to complete my deteriorating riding trousers and jacket.

A butcher's shop was located in the centre of the black market, a series of small huts pulled together under one large roof, refrigeration was not common in these lands with the meat stacked high on the counter side, as the flies circled with glee. The meat stays mainly field dressed, with the animals of cow and sheep either kept whole or cut lengthways hung from the rafters and sat on the counter tops. The red hues and fat marbled the meat with clear quality, the trick would be to find the fresh cuts. I had no way of cooking such large quantities but daydreamed of a healthy rib-eye and fries. I stood watching the bartering take place, the women filled their plastic bags to the brim, with all parts from hooves to heads.

Behind me, I heard the first deep slow blasts of an accordion and the guttural singing I had heard so often in films and on TV. I made a beeline for the source and in amongst the stalls of wolf hides, traditional boots and saddles sat a man and woman adorned in highly elaborate silk Dels. Perched on wood stalls they continued through their songs with unchanged expressions, both of them wore thick white makeup on their faces and deep red on their lips, they looked similar to the Japanese geisha without the vanity and servitude. Although I did not understand a single word they sang, images of the Steppe swung in front of me.

On the fourth night in Ulan, more people started to arrive, the first of which were two British riders coming in from the western border and had taken a truck over the last few days due to a heavy crash. They rode on large BMW 1200s, with one of the fellas coming unstuck, breaking several ribs and heavily damaging his bike. They achieved these accolades on the southern route, the route I was planning to take, albeit in the opposite direction. They had flagged down a truck who they had bartered to carry them to Ulan. They took stock on what had happened to them over the last few days and realized they had bitten off more than they could chew. They were beaten down and literally broken. The bikes were too heavy for any kind of practical purposes such as picking up the bike after a spill or controlling it at slow speeds. The bikes were yet to be unloaded but they had arranged for them to be taken straight to the workshop of a local bike mechanic. Their mood changed over a few days as they relaxed into the hostel and into Ulan, passing their anxieties and worries to me.

Next to arrive was a couple in a purpose built three hundred-thousand-dollar overland truck, the yellow elephant had come unstuck multiple times since leaving the west coast of America and the shaken look in the eyes of the driver told everything you needed to know. He was at the stage of questioning - why did I decide to do this? Am I cut out for this? How can I get out of this? Will I make it home?

Two nights before I planned to leave two young lads arrived from Germany on 1980s BMWs. After the usual exchange of stories the two lads, Demetri, me and the Bavarian retired to their yurt. It turned out it was the birthday of one of the German lads, so out came a set of party hats, cigars and whisky. We laughed deeply into the dark night, enjoying the brotherly love, as the whiskey burnt and warmed our throats.

On my final night in Mongolia, I sat behind Oasis next to an open fire allowing the glow to dull the great sky. I was with a ragtag bunch of dirt bags and vagabonds, we all had stories but chose to sit there silently letting this fleeting bond keep us content. I knew that I would probably never see or speak with any of them again and that was fine because I knew they were out there, somewhere, falling, crashing, breaking and getting back up to sit by another fire somewhere knowing they had earned every lick off heat that emanated from the flames. The glow of the fire was suddenly overrun by headlights of a bike pulling into the parking lot, a brand new and gleaming BMW 800. From the saddle hopped a middle-aged man, clad in the three-thousand-dollar adventure suit I had seen only once when planning my trip, just like the bike, him and his suit was spotless.

He stood in a gap of the circle surrounding the fire and blurted loudly in a brash American accent, 'Who's on the Yamaha?' Dutch nodded. 'I have one of those as well, great bikes. I have seven bikes out here, all this year's model.'

Contempt is not strong enough to describe the looks on the faces of the seated vagabonds, I cleared the silence.

'You live out here?' I pondered. 'Yeah, I work for one of the natural gas companies in the south. I've been out here for almost three years.

'Do you live in Ulan?' I quizzed, he nodded.

'Do you mind if I join y'all?'

Dutch shrugged and I smiled, the Bavarian and the Germans avoided eye contact and the mutual silence that until a moment ago was so sweet had turned sour.

'I'm off to bed,' Demetri said and stepped between me and Dutch and walked inside. I gave it a few and followed suit, falling asleep as tomorrow I headed out on the Steppe, heading back towards Russia and then onto Kazakhstan.

Mongolia is vast by anyone's estimation, at any one point you can look around and see nothing but dust as far as the eye could see, I might as well have been on mars. The riding was hard on the hands but the beating had its own rhythm that made it tolerable for an hour or so at a time. Then I would have to stop and shake life back into the extremities and make sure Tina was in one piece.

Just after my fourth hour of jackhammering across the landscape, I noticed the bags were no longer nestled against my back, I ran my hand across my lower back to find where they were, they had shifted back quite a way. I decided to stop. The ground was solid enough to hold the centre stand, so I stood her up and rested my helmet on the saddle. I first looked at the straps that were still firmly in place and the bracket holding the two jerry cans was still tight. I kneeled down next to the bike and saw the problem, the frame that held all my luggage and panniers and extra fuel had snapped on both sides, the only thing holding it all together were the straps. The crack in the metal had gone all the way through, the frame was fully disconnected. I rubbed my eyes in frustration and looked around. I unclipped one of the straps and the back of the bike that held all my luggage dropped to the floor, I hadn't long refuelled and it was clear the weight had become too much for the frame under the constant hammering. To keep myself smiling I noted on how beautiful the landscape was and how big it made the sky. Over the next hour, I tried multiple combinations of anchor points and gaffer tape but nothing really held, there was only one thing for it, to make a brew and think.

 I sat down on my jacket and quickly boiled water on my stove, adding the contents to my mug and teabag, I had no milk or anything to dunk but apart from these atrocities it was a delight to be out here. As I sat there just staring at the tapped frame I noticed a dust trail forming on the horizon from the east, it soon grew into a distinguishable outline of a large flatbed truck stacked high with wrapped goods. I watched as the truck pulled up next to me and the two men inside hopped out. The driver was the oldest of the two, with jet black hair neatly parted to the side with a cleanly shaved heavily wrinkled face similar to that of an old salty sailor, weathered to leather. The younger one wore a jacket and trousers heavily rolled at the cuffs and hem to make them fit. His skin was smooth and wore a constantly perplexed look, he missed a front tooth and his hair ran in all directions. None of us could exchange information verbally but the problem was clear with a simple point to the frame and the pile of luggage. The two men spoke to one another and the young one jumped back in the truck and grabbed some paper, on it drew thirty thousand, about two hundred US dollars.

'To fix?' I inquired with a bump of my hands, the older fella shook his head and patted the air in the direction to the west.

'Where? Ulgi?' I questioned, the old guy nodded again.

I couldn't believe my luck, Ulgi was the next big town and would hopefully be home to a welder to help me fix the bike. It was en route to the border so I extended my hand and shook on the agreement without any real thought, their nonchalant approach to this seemingly trivial problem silenced my anguish. The head honcho hopped back into the truck and backed it up against a natural embankment, to solve the problem that the bed of the truck lay four feet above the track, the younger one was ordered to the back of the truck and started to untie various ties holding the tarp over their load. I gave a hand and soon we had cleared enough space to fit Tina, with little effort these two men lifted Tina into the back. I fumbled around trying to help but the speed and effort that these men worked kept me at bay.

My disposable way of living in England and America had left me soft and wanting. The rugged world in which these men operated created a necessity on their hands and their mental skills to survive, to keep moving no matter what came their way. Had I regressed in my mental capacity with a life focused on a single skill? These men had to heal themselves, repair their vehicles and tools, sell their work, control their animals, adapt to the weather and answer any number of brutalities that came their way. It was easy for me to throw away and to order another online and search the solution instead of storing the steps within my own memory. With all their apparent skills, I pondered if my brain or my capacity were reduced compared to theirs. It stood to reason, with the very different lives with led. So the challenge then, was could I get it back? Like a lost language hidden in rusted tools, untouched skills and simple practicality.

The truck was reloaded with all the items around the bikes and on we continued towards Ulgi. From there I would ride to the border and for the second time be back into Russia, this time I would be in the Altai, or Gold Mountain as it translates in Mongolian. Onwards we bounced feeling the full effect of the corrugated track. There wasn't a spare seat for me so I sat hunched on the thin track that lay behind the two seats. My height was not advantageous and the constant pounding played havoc with my spine, but at least I was hauling in the right direction.

We stopped for a rest next to a gentle and shallow stream running along a bank that was home to three yurts. We entered the middle one, in the centre of the yurt stood a wood burning stove holding a large cast iron pan and a kettle. Around the outside was all the furniture they needed from a small crib to a delicate set of draws, the struts and furniture were heavily decorated in oranges and floral patterns. A small child, fat faced and red, slept under a blanket, tightly pulled up under her chin. I was instructed to sit down near the child sleeping, as the mother readied a pot on the stove. Although the sun was high in the sky the Yurt was very dark, albeit a few cracks of light here and there and the small doorway.

The lady prepared some dark meat on a large chopping board that must have been goat or mutton, along with some root vegetables they were added to the pre-heated pot in the middle. As they smouldered away she kneaded small balls of dough into a what looked like flatbread. She made them ever so thin then cut them into small strips, creating noodles. She timed their addition to the pot with silent confidence. I sat there in the warmth of the stove, the fire was fuelled by manure harvested from the herds outside. It emitted a wonderful earthy smell that filled the home.

I was handed a small bowl full of ingredients from the pot, it was dense and warm, the ideal meal for life of a nomad. My nomadic life may only be for a few months but I truly felt as one with these people, maybe not to the extent they would refer to me as a friend or exude any large amount of care other than what was needed to get me out of the mitts but enough to be extended the utilitarian need for a meal or a bed. As I sat there eating the deep bowl a little lamb meandered into the yurt and straight to the feet of the woman, she reached over and grabbed a bottle of milk and sat there feeding him. We all knew one day that animal would end up in the pot or succumb to the hunt of a wolf pack but the care that was extended and the happy existence the lamb lived showed the deep understanding these nomadic people had on their place within a delicate and interdependent ecosystem, an understanding I had largely lost from my own life.

We arrived in Ulgi in a little under forty-eight hours since my bike broke down and just as easily as they had picked me up the bike was welded back together and rebuilt and ready to roll. I was at a complete loss for what to do when my frame snapped yet to them it was nothing more than an average day in this part of the world. I felt angry but let myself off with a simple lesson learnt speech.

    Within thirty seconds of riding I was outside of the city limits and I was away, into the hills. The geology of the land showed clear traces of an ancient river bed, which created a dusty maze for me to navigate as I climbed high into a mountain pass. As I climbed the cloud base came closer and closer, feeling the air get wetter with every breathe, the dust darkened with the moisture content finally giving way to grass. I came to stop on a beautiful sweeping pass that looked as if it had been untouched by man, it was surreal to be here. I could see no further than five hundred meters or so due to the thick cloud I had climbed into, but it did nothing to the beauty of this place. If anything, it made it more special as it was mine and mine alone. This whole moment encapsulated perfectly what this adventure was about, simply just being out here, in the wild, with an untouched air and an undiscovered land.

    It wasn't long from leaving the pass when I came to the rim of a large sand bowl some two and a bit kilometres wide. The trail I was on disappeared into sand then reappeared on the opposing lip, the bowl held no discernible track or route to take yet down to my left I could see rocks lay strewn, lightly covered by sand. I guessed riding on rocks would give me better traction and a firmer surface to support me and Tina. I rolled over the edge and instantly the front tire started to sink. I gunned the throttle and stood up on my pegs, sand spat out behind. Standing was the best technique for tackling sand, or so I had read. I started to gain momentum and was able to make the half way point when, as gentle as a summer breeze I started to fly over my handlebars. I completed a full summersault landing flat on my bum, unhurt. Tina was still upright being held up by the sand.

'Stand up on sand they said,' I chuckled as I walked back to Tina.

Using the throttle to steer I was able to get going enough to make it up the other side and out the bowl. Proud of my Dakar skills I treated myself to some water. I unstrapped my boots and emptied them of the sand, the cool air around my toes felt almost sexual. The sand gave away again to damp dirt as the track carried me back into the sky.

The wet air started to reach through my layers causing me to shudder, the track led along the brown mountainside, reminding me greatly of North Wales. Soon the Steppe opened out beneath me and I rolled gently down the hillside into the landscape that reminded me of where I was, Western Mongolia.

In the distance a Yurt stood alone next to a small stream, the ground was deep green making the small white home stand out. I stayed high and far right of the Yurt as beyond the river was a herd of sheep and although I couldn't see them I knew there must be the Bankhar or the Mongolian Sheepdog. I had been warned of the voraciousness and their lack of fear for humans. My fear was soon realized as two came bounding across the slope directly at me, there large winter coats were still firmly in place making them look more like black bears than dogs. They barked and growled as they sprinted towards me. I tried to remain calm and avoid any sudden movements as the ground was wet and slippery, taking a spill would have made things far too interesting for this day or any other for that matter. The first to reach me came within a meter and ran alongside barking, the second went straight for my boot, I flung my foot forward catching him in the lower jaw, he persisted to take another bite so I swung again, this time I hit far harder than the first, causing me to swerve on the bike. I was able to connect with the bone of his jaw, he shook off the majority of the force, backed away and ran alongside for a further minute until they both gave up and watched me ride off into the distance.

    I rode on, focusing on the bike and the three meters in front of my wheels, as I dipped through hundreds of little streams from six inches to several feet wide. Now the dogs were gone I started having the time of my life, the engine roared, with water splashing everywhere, instantly turning to steam on my pipes and radiator, the big clouds of white steam that were constantly around my bike, made Tina look like a breathing dragon.

    We bounced and hopped our way over fifty kilometres of rough ground to the base of a steep track that climbed about six hundred meters straight up. The track was heavily scarred with the trucks and vehicles that had clambered their way up and down. I pulled to a stop and decided to assess my best route to take up the mountainside. I split the track into three, the first part was simply best to tackle straight on as much of the scree had compacted into a relatively smooth launch ramp that I hoped would get me to the mid-section, the middle looked by far the hardest part, it was the steepest and most heavily pitted part of the mountain. I planned to tackle it at an angle giving me the best traction but I ran the risk of going perpendicular to the mountain, creating a dangerous setup if I took a spill. The third section started with a dip then steepened to a gentle shoulder all the way to the top.

I went to put my headphones away in a muscle memory fashion, only to realize I hadn't had my music on all day. I laughed, tightened my helmet straps, clicked the buckles on my boots and was away.

The first stretch went according to plan as the low down torque of Tina came into its own, the speed I had gathered pitched me dangerously into the second stage. I hopped like a fat gazelle from rut to rut, my legs were sprayed open ready to catch a fall and all I could do was laugh, this was so much fun. I slipped and slid across this steep mountainside, before I knew it I was halfway through stage three and onto the shoulder. I climbed slowly to the top and flipped the stand out, looking back from where I had come.

I stood with the biggest smile on my face on my beautiful ascent. My summit celebrations were short lived as the downside of the mountain was just as steep as the way up. I pulled to the lip of the slope and flipped my visor up, the air was cold and fresh and wet, it filled me with confidence as I pulled the air deep down through my diaphragm into my legs. I placed my right foot onto the rear brake, she was already in first gear so I rolled over the edge. The mountainside sloped down and to my left, ending in a ravine. I chose my spot to my right and stayed fixed on that point with my gaze, to avoid drifting near the ravine. I forgot the front brake and slowly but surely we merrily bounced to the bottom of the hill. I would have earned zero points for grace but we had accomplished it, in one piece and upright.

The grass rolled flat for a few miles before it merged into a main track that led me to the border. The last few miles were nothing more than that god awful compacted corrugated dirt and dust. I pulled my chin around to take one last look. I had risen and fallen and risen again in Mongolia, I sparred with all of Mongolia and what she had to offer, the blunt blows and gentle jabs, the knockout blows and the congratulatory I had given it all hugs. Mongolia had won over me and the weather over her, a part of her lay deep inside me, down, down, down in the blackness, where it is raw and open, the place where my ancestors rest in amongst the stardust that creates us. There sat Mongolia, rumbling the guttural songs that I must never talk about, like an unwritten code of ethics.

All through this hard work, hard graft, tears, blood and sweat, I had spent a huge amount of energy leaving a large void inside of me, as I went further on this trip the emptiness and fatigue that had been spent was silently being filled by a true sense of worth, a strong stabilizing matter, holding me together for whatever would come over the hill or around the corner.

I read somewhere that the worst thing a man can do is be comfortable, I'd be lying if hadn't wished for Libby's hand, our bed, a home-cooked meal or fresh pair of pants but as I stood next to Tina at the Russian border, shuffling paperwork and showing the contents of my panniers, I suddenly noticed how much my shoulders ached. The deep dull pain I had in my hips, swelling around my ankle and the cracks in my bike frame but none of it mattered or bothered me because my sense of worth made me so deeply happy. I knew now and forever more I was untouchable. I had no clue on what lay ahead but I was going to get home, I knew it, nothing would change that. The panniers were repacked and my papers returned, I said farewell to Mongolia and for my second time I entered into Russia.

THE ALTAI

I passed through the high fenced compound that marked the Russian border and was immediately met with paved road, I would have kissed it if I wasn't so close to armed guards. The mountains ran out from the valley floor below, through dense pine, larch and fir, upwards to where the snow took over. A single empty road collared the dark brown river brimming with sediment, meandering its way through the landscape, some two hundred meters below. It was simply magical, pleasing and joyous to be riding free on this road.

I had spent no time analysing this two-day ride between Mongolia and Kazakhstan yet the Altai turned into one of the most beautiful moments of the expedition. The weather remained a perfect mix of blue and warmth, I only had a little further to ride as I had given myself a high buffer for the border crossing and the last few hundred kilometres of Mongolia, but I had crossed back into Russia in less than an a few hours putting me firmly ahead of schedule.

I bumbled along in such grace that I overshot the turning to where I would be staying by nearly twenty kilometres, I swung round and drove back to the turning of the mountain lodge and my home for the night. It was a waypoint given to me by another adventurer during the planning stage marked simply as 'hotel'. What it turned out to be was a small mountain farm run by a lovable old couple.

I pulled in next to the main building that occupied one-fifth of the stone walled courtyard, the rest of the space was mainly open albeit a large workshop, covered machinery and a pig pen. Where lazy spotted lumps sniffed at my boots and the bike.

What I assumed to be the owner came and greeted me as I unloaded the bike, I could see that one side of the frame had snapped again and needed another repair. I stopped my inspection as I shook hands with Yuri, he was a potbellied man well into his sixties with large earth grown hands and a strong back. He looked happy to see me and me, him. I pointed to the frame and the crack that had reopened, he acknowledged it was a 'yes' along with some hand gestures to signal me to take it apart for him. I unpacked my tool roll and sat down on the gravel to start removing the rack from the rear frame. Yuri stopped me midway and beckoned me to follow him, we walked across the yard to an Old Russian Military Zil Truck, on the bed was a camper kept in beautiful condition. It was Yuri's pride and joy, through his broken English he explained he and his wife would still go north in it every year to hunt and fish and enjoy the woods. He unlatched and untied every box showing the thoughtful and well-prepared contents from shovels and snares to replacement parts, like my grandfather's tool, shed, it was clear he had spent years working, grafting, saving and fixing to make this dream possible.

I went back to removing the rear rack and frame, allowing my back to warm in the early summer sun. I set my jacket down and flicked my braces with my thumbs to the fact that although she was falling apart, Tina had got me here, albeit, in three unintended pieces. I took the two parts of the frame and followed Yuri into his workshop that was dark and oily and held the means to keep everything going. I smiled and took two steps back at the rudimentary welder that Yuri used. He attached a large crocodile clip to a bare junction box and the other to a large metal rod, striking and earthing it he made a connection and began to weld. He put a spare rod into the tubing of the frame to add strength and closed the weld. Whether I was tired, complacent, simply stupid or a combination of the three, I went to grab the frame to inspect Yuri's work, giving no thought to the fact that it might be hotter than the fires of hell. Yuri stopped me at the last second in disbelief at what I tried to do, he smiled at my schoolboy error and beckoned me outside.

We went into the main house and he showed me to my room, small and simple, a bed, a simple lamp upon a little table and a little wooden stool. It was perfect and again for one night only it would become my home. Yuri let me use his kettle to boil some water and settled down with a cup of soup and the obligatory noodles.

Morning rose just as it had on every other day and I took to rebuilding Tina, I paid little attention to my hands as they lashed down my luggage and secured the panniers. I forced Yuri into a photo of him and Tina, I hugged him and rode on, I was slowly learning that the act of helping your fellow man is not an event to cheer or celebrate but a basic need of existence.

KAZAKHSTAN

I had entered the largest landlocked country on earth and just as the scenery had changed from the Wetlands of Mongolia to the Mountains of the Altai I was now in a dusty city with no want to stay any longer than I had to. Starting in 1949 the USSR started as series of 456 nuclear tests about one hundred and fifty kilometres west of the city, leading to huge amounts of cancer and births defects within Semey and the surrounding towns.

I caught a few hours' sleep and moved quickly on to Astana, Kazakhstan's capital before first light. It was a pretty long punt to hit in one day but with my head down and the joy of being in a new country and time zone the eight hundred kilometres passed with little worry. With the huge resources of natural gas, petroleum, iron, gold and uranium Astana is a modern city by any standard. It hadn't been around long enough to have the grit of New York or the history of London or the beauty of Paris but the influx of money was very apparent. Just head over to the KazMunayGas building, which is the state-owned oil and gas company and you'll be confronted by a behemoth, a monolith of human placed stone.

This land was as alien to me as Russia or Mongolia, yet the roads were built to ride and blast, dead and true. They were far better than those of Russia, with the occasional abrupt end to the asphalt, continuing on dirt. Sometimes these would lead me to second guess my route, as sometimes the road ahead often looked ominous and menacing, the badlands, a home of misfortune and strife, yet a solid swig of water and a deep breath kept me moving forward.

I had inputted a very important waypoint in Astana given to me by the British fellas in Ulan Bator, it was a steak restaurant, and referred to as "a bloody good one at that". I was able to get a room around the corner in a small hotel with a gated parking lot. I treated myself to a full shower and shampoo and put on the only collared shirt I had, I went to put on my jeans when I admitted to myself the state in which they resided was just too awful, so a quick hand wash in the hotel room sink and a blitz over with the hairdryer had me looking like Bond, well, maybe the guy that changes the oil in his DB5.

Off I sauntered towards the restaurant, but the only thing I had not factored was the heat. I was simply too excited about the idea of eating a steak, combined with the thick flannel shirt I was a mess. In order to not draw attention to myself I chose a spot in the far corner to sweat out all my bodily fluids. The steak came with a big bottle of red and a rich chocolate dessert, perfectly seasoned and cooked beautifully rare. The meat was like butter, the wine was dark and opulent and the dessert was enough to send me in a beautifully deep food coma.

I awoke the following day with a very sensitive head being stabbed by bright sunlight coming through cracks in the curtain. With a large bottle of water I wandered the few blocks near my hotel allowing life to trickle back, as I explored the churches and back streets of the city.

Leaving Astana, the road split and it was as if the world ran out in every direction as far as I could see. It looked infinitely sparse, the heat was intense so I removed the lining of my jacket to keep cool. Yet the real misery of the heat came at every fuel stop. Each time a thick dense fog made up of thousands of tiny little flies, would consume the space around my face. My first fuel stop I removed my helmet and the flies got in my eyes, mouth, ears and nose, they were no bigger that gnats making them extra hard to swat, the heat kept me sweating and the flies coming in a torrent. I rushed to fill the bike and get my helmet back on, yet even with my helmet on they would find a way into my nose and eyes.

I had got used to being in a state of homoeostasis when I was on the bike, not really needing rest, food, the toilet or much water. I was halfway through the day's ride when I realised with a great urgency I needed a number two, the road was straight in both directions giving me certainty the coast was clear. I hunkered down next to a large concrete statue of some country leader or hero, holding onto a corner post of the giant 70ft statue I was able to lean back and get the required clearance. There is something ever so fulfilling about taking a poop in the open air, however, this sense of primal freedom was soon lost when a coach load of Kazaks passed by. There I was holding on to their national monument taking a large poo, there was little I could do other than continue, as moving might cause unwanted plastering of my garments.

As the day went on the road started getting worse, the road looked like it had been bombarded for a whole year by mortar rounds. It was difficult to get any rhythm and anything about thirty miles an hour left me no time to react to the two-foot-deep craters. On the smaller ones I found that I could punch the throttle on the edge allowing me to skip over them without bottoming out the suspension, but the larger ones would require me to weave around them in a dangerous dance.

The constant weaving was tiring and the excessive nothingness that consumed the horizon in every direction created a twilight zone like experience which had me babbling by the end of the day. The physicality of the road was playing havoc on my hips and knees, sharp pains ran up each leg and flank and sometimes ending in my shoulders. For the first few hours, I just told myself that they simply weren't there then it got too much. I rummaged for some pain killers in my bags only to remember that I had given them to the two brits in Ulan. I decided to rest a little more often, lying flat on the dirt allowed the weight of my body to unwind.

I finally reached the border town that entered back into Russia for the final time. Kazakhstan had been a quiet country, I had kept mostly to myself. I seemed to have exhausted all of my negative thoughts and was content with just being in the present. My mind would sometimes circle back to ideas of home and the life ahead with Libby but for the most part, I was simply here.

I had spent two months on the road and my life had been played out, both the reruns and the future episodes. I was not even thinking about how to ride a bike anymore, I just appeared at my end location with bags in my hand ready to stow away next to my bed.

The zig-zagging of the last five hundred or so pushed me straight into a deep sleep, skipping dinner, it was always in the morning I would learn how tired I was the night before. If I was in exactly the same position that I went to sleep in, then I knew I was close to exhaustion and this morning fell firmly into that category. I noticed the faded curtains and the cheap plastic table, the heat that was consuming the room and that my bum had slipped through the broken slats of the bed, almost touching the ground. Light from the moon filled the room, sunrise was still a few hours away. Today I would cross the border into Russia, two days later I would be in Ukraine and shortly after that, it didn't seem real, and then… I would be in Europe; a stone's throw from home.

There was little traffic as I pulled into my final Kazakh checkpoint before I went back into Russia. Little order seemed to be in play as we milled around the dusty square waiting to be called to a small hut for a paperwork check. A small couple well into their seventies came across and with a nervous tone spoke in Russian to me, I replied with what I was doing, saying as much as I could with my hands. Maybe it was arrogant to presume what they were asking about.

Soon it was my turn to go to the hut. I adorned the smile that had got me out so much trouble and laid my passport and documents on the small wooden shelf that sat below the officer's window. Behind the glass sat a young kid with huge excitement in his eyes as my British passport caught his gaze. I was now used to border guards running off with my paperwork, and as he left his seat I turned to find that the old couple were once again by my side. The woman moved over and wrapped her arm around mine, patting my back as if to check me over. She turned to her husband and kept chatting as we stood there in the sun. Only a few minutes passed when from across the court came an older guard, fully armed. He moved slowly as he tucked his shirt into his trousers, he opened the door of the hut and went inside. Both of them exited the hut and came over to me, I was ready for the 'follow me wave', and right on cue, he indicated that I needed to follow him.

I was led down a long white corridor of the main building and at the end sat the purpose of the soldier's commands. It was a jail cell, a clichéd, barred jail cell consisting of a bench and seatless toilet, the guard stepped aside and pointed into the cell. I went cold. I was expecting a cup of tea not this.

'No,' I commanded. 'What have I done?'

He did not answer but took a step closer, he wasn't afraid of me.

'I am not going in there until you tell me what I have done,' I said, snarling my jaw and gaze directly into his eyes.

This was wrong, it was off kilter, if I had wronged them then why not just kick me out of Kazakhstan? 'I'm good with your country,' I thought. We stood there in silence neither of us wanting to back down. My temper had neglected that another guard had approached from down the corridor. He put a hand on my shoulder giving me a start. I turned to see who it was. The new guard, a younger man, pointed to the cell. 'Sit in there, go.' His English was slow and forced.

'Tell me why I am here,' I said.

Fearing what might happen if they suddenly decided I was a difficult person that needed to be taught some manners, I decided to enter the cell. The first guard closed the cell door and turned a key letting the heavy lock confirm my position. They both moved back down the corridor and out of sight.

I ran my hands over my pockets to get my cell phone, only to realise I had left it in my tank bag, I had nothing on me. They had my paperwork and passport, my phone and emergency device were on my bike along with my cash, food and water. I tried to rationalise why I was here, talking to myself in an attempt to calm the obvious thoughts that were running through my brain. Maybe my visa had expired, no, that wasn't it. Maybe it was something I had done. Was I rude to anyone? No, I was in a jovial mood because I was only a week's ride away from Europe. It was probably money they were looking for, I had a thousand US dollars in the bottom of one my panniers. If they hadn't already found it, rummaging through my kit, I would offer it up when someone returned.

I sat, waiting for someone to return, hours passed and still nothing. I called down the corridor multiple times but no one replied. I resorted to running scenarios in my mind if those two guards came back and wanted to give me a kicking, would I fight, or simply protect myself? I was clearly the bigger of the three but they had weapons and training. I did have my bike jacket and trousers on and if I held my forearms over my head the padding in the elbow and arms would offer some protection. All I needed to do was fend them off or try and make a run for it.

I waited but still no one came. I evolved through every emotion. I thought back to the story of Demetri and his stint in Northern Siberia for a few months. I laughed at the fact at least I would be warm. I had no way of keeping time but I guessed I had been there for about ten hours when a woman approached carrying a wad of paperwork, her face was twisted, old and naturally angry, a mere oil painting compared to the bastards that had put me in here. She unlocked the cell and sat beside me. The fact she came alone and left the cell door open was either an insult or an opportunity to make a run for it, but where would I run? I was inside a barracks that sat inside a military border between Kazakhstan and Russia, so I sat there and watched the events play out in front of me.

She set the stack of paperwork on my lap and followed the action with a simple command, 'You sign.' I flitted through the paperwork, it was all in Russian Cyrillic, all fifty or so pages. Was she mad? I was never going to sign this or anything else, I still hadn't been told what I had done and now I had to sign a huge undefined document.

'I am not signing this.' I was shaking. 'I need my medicine, on motocicle, medicine, for me.' I tapped my chest. She nodded as if she agreed, then stood, locked the door behind her and left the way she came.

An hour or so passed and the troll-faced woman returned, again opening the door and sitting next to me. I stood and she commanded me to sit. I explained my legs hurt and needed to move, in reality, my veins were bursting with adrenalin, fear, exhaustion and confusion.

She pointed to the stack of paper. 'You sign.'

'I… don't… know… what it says, I am not signing something I have any idea what it says.'

She looked perplexed as if it was perfectly agreeable for a person to blindly sign a military document in a language they only knew how to say hello and thank you.

'Sit down,' she commanded her voice raised in a harsh bark.

I felt a sense of pride with her agitated state, finally, I was sharing the wealth of anguish. I reined myself in by thinking of the bigger picture and sat back down.

'I will not sign this; I do not understand what it means. I have one thousand dollars, you can have, I go?' I tapped my jacket pocket. I wouldn't be surprised if they had already found the stash, maybe Tina had been dismantled and was on the black market already. She shook her head at the bribe.

'Okay, we bring translator.' She concluded. I started to really panic.

Time disappeared along with the sun and all my sense of reason, I sat with my back against the wall and brought my knees to my chest, my knee pads gave my forehead a nice pillow to watch the hours go by. The cell had no window but it must have now been night time, the whole place had fallen quiet, even my thoughts. I had given up trying to reason what the hell was going on and started to build up my armour, ready for whatever might come towards me both mentally and physically. My train of thought was suddenly broken when there was the sound of a helicopter approaching, it caused me to go to full alert, was that for me? I couldn't let them move me anywhere at least without my phone or emergency beacon. I agreed with myself to fight to the last to make sure that I would get hold of those connections to the outside world.

The troll and one of the original guards appeared at my cell and indicated for me to follow. I went down the corridor, turning away from the exit and into a large room. Inside was the other border guard, the junior soldier who I originally handed my paperwork to, a senior officer with elaborate regalia on both epaulettes and a woman in civilian clothing looking just as confused as me. I was ordered to sit down next to the woman, which I did. The woman opened her mouth and started speaking fluent English. 'There appears to be a problem with your paperwork,' she explained.

'What?'

'They say you don't have the right paperwork to ride a motorcycle in this country,' she continued, her voice shaking slightly.

I looked at the troll. 'Yes. Yes, I do, I gave it to him.' I pointed at the junior guard in the corner of the room. He presented my passport and visa and the small white piece of paper I had been given when I entered the country. 'See there is everything,' I said, my voice raising. I was getting angrier. 'What was wrong, what's not there?'

The translator explained my rant to the room. The troll took the white piece of paper and laid it out on the table. 'You need signature,' she said, pointing at a small box on the bottom left.

'Whose signature? Mine?' I probed.

The lady again translated then answered 'No the border guard in which you entered must sign when you enter Kazakhstan!'

'How is this my fault? You fucking.... you guys didn't do your job!'

'You must pay a fine.' One of the guards said.

I laughed at the ceiling. 'Shit, you just want money. How much?'

No discussion was held, with an immediate number being passed to the translator, 'Five thousand dollars.' The woman sheepishly answered.

I was about to laugh again when something stopped me. 'Can I transfer you the money once I am in Russia?'

A discussion was held with the pompous prick in the corner. It was agreed, bank account details were written on a piece of paper and handed to me. The troll explained that if I failed to pay they would send a summons. I agreed and tried to look as concerned as possible.

I was led back outside and taken to my bike. I didn't spend any time checking my kit other than my tank bag which appeared to be complete. I fired up the engine and rode through the gate into Russia. I was elated I was out of there, the only problem left was that I had three hundred kilometres to ride to the next city and it was now in the middle of the night coupled with a cold heavy rain. I didn't want to ride at night, the roads were dangerous with potholes and god knows else what, plus I was exhausted from what had just happened. I decided to find somewhere to sleep until first light, it couldn't have been more than three or four hours away. I didn't have to search far until I found an old bus shelter, covered in corrugated iron. There was a basic wooden bench inside, so I pulled Tina up next to the bench, creating a wind break. I kept my helmet on and curled up on the bench, I put my hands into my pockets for some added warmth only to find the slip of paper I'd been given to pay my fine, with a smile I pressed the paper into a muddy puddle under then bench and slipped into a cold and wet sleep. It didn't take much to wake at first light.

RUSSIA…THIRD TIME LUCKY

The distance to Saratov was tough, I couldn't quite comprehend what had happened. I had to stop myself deconstructing my actions over the last thirty-six hours. My energy levels went to an ethereal place, keeping me going until I hit the city walls, surely enough I kept moving, the weather was clear and the sun gentle and through countless yawns and big breaths I had made it.

I was sat at some lights when two motorcycles pulled up next to me. One was a redheaded Harley guy, sporting a long ponytail and beard, he wore no helmet and showed me a huge sign of appreciation for Tina and the dirt that covered her flanks. On the other side was a young kid on a Japanese sports bike, he remained silent and cool, revving the engine to embolden his image.

The lights had not yet changed when the kid gunned it, straight out into the junction in some form of bravado, straight into the side of a minivan. My eyes grew with disbelief at what this kid had done. I looked at the redheaded Harley guy with eyes as wide as milk bottle tops. He just laughed and rode round the commotion that had now formed. I rolled slowly forward then got off to walk towards the kid who was now standing next to his broken rocket. I was so exhausted from last night's excursions in jail that the only thought that went through my head was 'How selfish does this prick want to be? Does he not understand I need a hotel and a shower? You my friend are an utter prick!' Then it dawned on me that was my first foray with a jail, was a military checkpoint in Kazakhstan. This was absurd, me in a *jail*! I still cried watching the *Lion King*. With slow deep huffs I began to laugh like a maniac, still walking towards the downed biker, I must have looked insane. Soon the laughter was too much and I just laughed uncontrollably, I couldn't even bring myself to ask if he was alright, I just stood next to him laughing with tears running down my cheeks. I managed to raise a thumb, which he copied and back I walked to my bike just laughing away.

In the centre of town, I found a large corporate hotel that looked more glamorous than anything I had seen all trip. They even had air conditioning, a car park, a reception desk and wi-fi. Wow, this place was swanky. Covered in shit, tears, dirt, dust, dead bugs, slobber, tarmac, oil and petrol I approached the front desk, this was the first time I had taken my helmet off since leaving Kazakhstan.

'I need a room,' I blurted.

'Sure. Sir, just to let you know our rooms are rather expensive,' she said in perfect English.

'Good' I said, 'Because my friend is paying, his name is Visa. Also, do you sell chicken club sandwiches?'

'Yes we do, they are on the room service menu.'

'Fantastic, I'll have four please.'

'Four?'

'Yes, four, and a beer for each.'

'Will friend be paying?'

'Yes.'

I was handed my room keys and made my way upstairs. Inside the room I couldn't believe my eyes, it was an actual double bed. I hadn't seen one of these monsters for months. My food and beer arrived and was gone in four large breathes as I fell asleep for close to sixteen hours.

UKRAINE

I headed down my final road in Russia that brought me into Ukraine. I was more than elated, I now had Russia, Kazakhstan and Mongolia behind me. Whilst Ukraine wasn't officially in the EU, it felt so close to home I could taste it.

The queue for the border was about a mile long, full of large articulated lorries and heavily packed vans and trucks. I pulled up and assumed my place in line. I had been waiting about twenty minutes noticing the queue hadn't moved an inch, when a bold bowling ball of a man sauntered over, whilst not in official or military uniform, he held himself with a fair amount of importance. He sported a gold watch and a clean well-sized leather jacket. He made a beeline for me, grinning all the way, he shouted something to me, most of which I couldn't understand yet I did hear something about tea. I started walking towards him but he sent me back to bring my bike. I wasn't quite sure how this was going to work out as he was on foot, and I had no room to carry him, so at walking pace I moved down the whole line until we were at the front of the queue. I looked around for signs of tea yet none arose. Suddenly the man blasted a piercing wolf whistle over to the guards, who then waved me over to the checkpoint. I turned to my new friend and thanked him, he then handed me a business card, black and matte, with silver type that read "Hollywood Hotel – Luhansk".

'My Brother owns the hotel, you stay, I call ahead.'

'Sure thing,' I agreed, almost meaning it.

I headed to the border guard and was quickly through the checkpoint and into Ukraine. I had no clue who my gold watch wearing man was but he definitely made my life easy, probability pointed to him being a member of the mafia that was very prevalent in Ukraine.

Mafia and police corruption were the two main stories I heard from travellers passing thru Ukraine, usually highly negative, involving theft or the continuous stopping by the police on whatever trumped up charges they created to extort money from tourists. Yet if this man were Mafia, I couldn't have been more pleased.

I arrived in Luhansk after a short ride, yet I was unable to secure any lodgings. This time the rejection was based on capacity rather than appearance and so I decided to check out the brother's hotel. I figured I could roll up and make an assessment and if it felt wrong then I would roll on to somewhere else. By now my threshold of 'too dodgy for me to stay' was pretty high. I had slept rough in yurts, next to Tina on benches, in a truck, in shacks and in a stranger's homes so when I pulled up outside this marble-fronted mansion I was heavily surprised. It seemed almost too good to be true, so in I lugged, stinking and covered in dirt approaching the black velvet front desk.

'You must be Paul,' said the blonde receptionist, her English was fantastic.

'Yes… yes, I am' I replied.

I started to feel very self-conscious of the state I was in, I hadn't shaved in a while and my facial hair grew akin to an old china man's testicle or so I had heard.

'How much?' I said.

'Oh nothing it is for you; we like to host people from England, it is our privilege.'

Well shit me, this was going to be awesome, unless I awoke with a kidney removed.

I was shown to my room and boy, what a room it was. The bathroom was all black with an oversized claw footed bath in the centre, the bed was gigantic and beyond anything I had ever seen with the hundred or so cushions that sat on top. The sheets were black silk and the pillows filled with a thick down. Behind the bed was a huge portrait of Marilyn Monroe made from tiny tiles. The portrait covered the whole wall all the way to the border of the eighteen-foot ceiling. I didn't want to touch anything. I was shown around and explained that everything was free from the minibar and I was not to hold back, she closed the door behind her and left me to my own devices.

I quickly broke into a dance with the luck I had run into, the clattering of my large boots covered the noise of the door reopening, only when I heard, 'Sorry I forgot to mention breakfast is from 8 a.m.' Embarrassed, I just nodded and again she left.

I latched the door closed and danced my way to the bathtub. I hadn't had a bath since leaving Boston so I was ecstatic to get the tub hot and bubbly. I put the plug in and turned the tap, with some large bangs and groans the dirtiest brown water emptied from the pipes straight into the bath tub. I stood trying to reason with myself that I should have a bath in the water, but my lure for a hot soak wasn't that strong. Instead, I got into the shower over in the corner and washed the world away, I used some shampoo for what looked like the first time, as the water ran black.

I left Luhansk in the late morning after a lazy breakfast of eggs and bacon on the roof deck of the hotel. My riding style had changed; I wasn't rushing to prep the bike or pound the road in the early hours. I simply trundled often riding nestled into my bag on the back rack with a hand on my thigh and right hand pushing down only with its weight keeping me at a psychedelic fifty miles per hour.

Ukraine was a pretty place with beautiful gothic architecture, and rolling hills. The riding days were short from here on out and I was mad that I should have listened to myself earlier, riding short days took a huge amount of stress out of me. I felt free to enjoy a cup of coffee and watch the world go by and marvel at my Triumph.

Tina would stand by my side looking like a complete badass, my panniers were beaten and scratched and her belly was covered in dirt. Dead bugs were everywhere and had been the major part of my diet for the last six weeks, if being covered in dirt made me feel so at ease, I'd never wash again.

On one stretch of road I could see two police officers waiting by their car, I could taste their joy when they clocked me. I pulled up next them remembering the advice Dutch had given me. 'Stay on the road,' he'd said. 'It blocks other traffic and they will soon get frustrated and let you on your way.'

I prayed Dutch was not just bullshitting as I came to a stop in the middle of the lane and pulled my visor. With a big thumb up I implored I had no clue on what this guy wanted from me, even though the rubbing off his fingers clearly meant cash. I just sat there grinning enthusiastically at this cop whilst the traffic built behind me. It took all of half a second for the honking to begin, like a great orchestra I let the honking build to a crescendo until the officers had no choice but to wave me on. Their faces angered with me spoiling their scheme. Thanks, Dutch.

The next day I pulled into a service station ready to fill Tina. Like an old craftsman I pottered between the bags and straps and the routine I had created to refuel, with steady confident hands I removed my helmet looping it over the right mirror. I twisted the bars to the left allowing me to push the tank bag forward exposing the fuel cap, I unlocked the cap, removed the key and sat it upside down on the seat. I gazed into the tank checking no debris sat on the rim that could be potentially pushed down into the tank, even if nothing was there I would still run my finger around to double check. Most petrol stations required you to pay in advanced, to keep overspend down I would give them a small amount each time and repeat the process until Tina was full. I would replace the nozzle into the pump allowing air bubbles to surface and pop before I replaced the tank cap. I would clean the tank with the side of my glove to make sure no dirt got onto the underside of my tank bag as I found this was an easy to scratch the paint. This was my routine and I was militant on its order making sure the life blood reached Tina just as I wanted.

In Ukraine and Russia, due to a throwback of the communist era, many petrol stations had men that would fill the tank for you. It upset me immensely as the goons fumbled and clattered and poured fuel everywhere. One such moment occurred outside of Volgograd, the filler was mid conversation with his co-worker when I pulled in. I unclipped the tank bag and removed the cap and let him at it as I went inside to get some water. I was stood at the till when I looked over at the kid filling my tank, to see he had continued his conversation with his pal, ceasing attention on filling Tina, who was long full causing fuel to pour over everything, including the seat, the bag, all coming together in a large puddle beneath the bike.

'Hey,' I called out, but my alert went unheard behind the glass. I grabbed my change and marched outside. 'Hey.' The kid looked up, disgruntled that I had broken him from his conversation. I marched towards him in large heavy steps with an arm out in front pointing at the puddle, he soon clocked on to what I was upset about and pulled the nozzle up into the air, yet he still kept his hand on the trigger spraying fuel all over my bags and panniers. He released and stood back. Tina stood there glistening with fuel in the midday sun.

'You fucking moron,' I muttered as I walked straight past him to the pile of tissue sat on the pump behind. I dabbed and blotted, pushing tissue into the cracks in hope to spare damage from the corrosive liquid. Since then I kept the process to myself, even tipping the pump boys to keep them happy and away from Tina.

Tina had grown into something beyond a machine, she was a key, a key to a door full of so much wonder and excitement. She held me down where the worms squirmed and the breeze ran, I couldn't hide from the rain, the wind, the snow or the sun, my skin cracked and glistened with whatever came my way. This was how it was meant to be, in a car I were disjointed and aloof, alone and isolated from the world around me. Tina carried me and all my belongings from border to border, from trouble to trouble, she burbled and roared, never stopping, she pushed me to move further. I was indebted to her, I had to care for her in a utilitarian way, like a shepherd to a dog. Whilst she was a tool for my work, without her I would not have met Svet or Anna, partied in Nashville or been looked after by the mafia in Ukraine. Her only downfall was that she had only one purpose and that was to move, sometimes sideways when the road got wet but mostly forward. I would never say goodbye to her, she would one day be sat in the garage of my daughter or son and then onto their childre. She had become my friend and guardian.

I was halfway through my routine at a corner fuel stop, some two hours away from Kiev, when a rumble from behind grew, a deep bubbling. I looked around to see a dark green and filthy Bentley Speed Six, over twelve feet long with the majority of its length taken with its broad and giant nose, giant spoked wheels and absurdly small windscreen. It looked more like an old biplane without wings than a car. Sat in the cockpit were two old fellas with the obligatory goggles and flat caps, oil and dirt lining their cheeks. They pulled up rather quickly to the fuel pump as myself and petrol station staff looked on in disbelief. These beasts usually sat dying in a museum somewhere and here it was, covered in as much soil as Tina.

The co-pilot had all but got to the back of the car when a second one pulled in followed by a beautiful and petite Alfa Guilia, a 70s Bug, a Mustang, an old Porsche 911 and Model T with wooden spoked wheels, plus a plethora of other wonderful classic cars. You simply couldn't make this stuff up, five days ago I was in jail in Kazakhstan and now I am in between millions of pounds' worth of classic cars, each with the Monte Carlo Rally red and yellow style plaques reading "Peking to Paris 1907 to 2013". Soon a bunch of support vehicles pulled in with tired and bewildered mechanics and odd-jobbers, running round performing a myriad of duties. I sat on Tina side saddle watching all the chaos.

'And what are you doing?' came a voice from behind me.

'Who me?' I smiled.

'Yeah, where have you come from?

'Boston.'

'On that? Strewth, I'm Bill.'

'I'm Paul nice to meet you.' He extended a filthy hand, it matched my own. We shook.

'Want some water?' Bill asked.

'Sure,' I said.

Bill was a foul-mouthed Aussie driving an old Ford Mustang. He explained their endeavour, listing their route from Peking then onto the Great Wall of China – Inner Mongolia – Gobi Desert – Outer Mongolia – Ulaan Baatar – Telmen Lake – Russia – Novosibirsk – Omsk – Tyumen – Samara – Ukraine – Kiev – Lviv – Slovakia – Kosice – Bratislava – Austria – Schladming – Switzerland – Gstaad – France – Troyes – Paris.

It was a mixture of glamorous hotels and bloodied knuckles keeping these classics running on the roads. From snapped axels to a very sad death of one of the members in a very unfortunate car accident in Siberia, they had literally been through the ringer yet they all shared a smile and kept an eye on the prize of finishing the rally in Paris in a month's time.

'Where are you heading?' Bill asked.

'Kiev today then onto Lviv the following day.'

'So are we, where you staying?'

'Haven't a clue, I'll figure that out when I get into town.' I answered.

'Well here, take this and come and join us for beer and grub.'

He handed me a pass on a lanyard, it was a white badge that read "Mechanic".

'It will get you into our dinner hall tonight, the food is pretty decent.' He explained.

Once again I couldn't believe where my story was going, someone was definitely looking over me.

'Thanks, Bill, that's awesome, it will be a nice change to super noodles and bottled water.'

He walked back into his group, sharing the day's stories as the fuel pumps worked overtime.

I stood watching the visible bond amongst the competitors, envious of their brotherhood. Whilst I was emboldened with my self-reliance and the fact I had no fancy support crew following me, I would have been lying if I hadn't wished for a brother by my side to share in the glory and hardships.

I rubbed my thumb across the clean plastic of my meal token and tucked it safely into my chest pocket. I caught a few looks and waves from some of the other competitors but kept my distance not wanting to impose as I saddled up and rode on.

Once in my hostel in Kiev, which was a dive even by my standards, hidden in a back street amongst graffiti covered grocery stores and derelict buildings. By now though these type of dwellings were becoming the norm, it fulfilled a need, nothing more. I quickly got tidied away then got out my oiliest shirt and my only pair of jeans that were now like Velcro. I had to peel hard to fold out my outfit, each oil stain was a medal, each rip was a memory of trouble and the smell was a reminder I just needed to wash them more often.

I arrived at the river where their five-star hotel resided. They had made a heavily branded court in front of the hotel set aside for all the classic cars. I wore my mechanic's badge around my neck yet as I pulled up to the gate the hotel staff wanted nothing to do with me and had me park on the pavement away from my four-wheeled counterparts. Tina to me was the Oscar winner, she was British royalty, the most badass bitch around, but next to these cars from as early as the turn of the last century she appeared nothing more than mediocre to the crowds that had formed outside the hotel. I wasn't getting any attention, the attention that I had gotten so used to receiving. I was the solo motorcycle guy going around the world, it landed me in jail and on Russian TV, that all so familiar chip was firmly back on my shoulder as I stomped and swaggered across the court and through the cars to the hotel bar.

Bill was nowhere to be seen and without Tina for context I was a very dirty kid that was getting odd looks from the other drivers. I soon realised I was sporting the mechanic badge but not the black polo shirt and trousers, the uniform of the mechanic. I was getting redder in my cheeks and feeling very self-conscious so I made a beeline for the bar, hoping that a strong dose of whisky would settle me. I found a narrow stool between a wall and a massive American guy sporting the clichéd Ralph Lauren shirt and loafers. Bill later told me he was some oil billionaire from the Texas or some such state. He seemed to have a natural disdain for anyone that held less greed than he did and even after finding out our commonality of adventure he still forced nothing more than a grunt from his lips. As I stood at the bar, others pushed me aside to access the drinks without a single word.

I simply was not bred to swing with these cats, so I focused on the booze, yet even the whisky was helping in all the wrong ways. It filled me with confidence that caused me to spew stories and reasons why they should accept me, loudly I blurted, to anyone that would listen.

'I have a bike, I am going round the world, more miles than you'll ever know,' I blurted. 'Hey you own the Porsche or whatever right, is it solid?' I slurred.

My need for friendship was overwhelming any chance I had at making friends. I gave myself one more whisky and made my way back to Tina. I caught my hip on a table on the way out making a large bang, it was the most acknowledgement I had received all evening. I was angry at myself - why I was I so hell bent on getting acceptance from a bunch of rich old men and women? I wanted to cry and hide somewhere. Whenever I wanted something to work I would fuck it up, I would over commit and scare people away, my cheeks grew redder and I was close to tears.

I knew I had been on the road for a long time, on my own and I had been through a lot and the idea of having someone to shoot the shit with was highly appealing, yet I knew 99% of these folks were not the people I needed. People treated money it two ways, the first was a status symbol, I'm better than you because I have more than you. It's the basis of a capitalist society, the other group is the one that realizes money is an access card to do the things that truly mean something, on an intrinsic level, like starting a company to enable positive change, starting a foundation, or being able to afford the time to see the world and understand her a little better before time is up. For the majority of the cats here, this was a status symbol, they publicised their daily exploits, lauded their expensive choices to overcome any sense of hardship and adventure. It just wasn't me but I needed someone to talk to and laugh with and it outweighed my better judgement.

I walked across the parking lot where the beautiful cars were parked, back toward Tina. Staggering as I went, getting angrier at myself, causing me to quicken my pace so I could get on the bike and the hell out of there. As I turned the corner to where Tina was parked, I realized she had been surrounded by a group of the drivers along with Bill.

'Here he is,' Bill exclaimed.

I had to steady myself as the tears were sat in the ducts ready to flow. A couple of deep breaths and a smile kept the tears at bay. I struggled to remain calm as the questions and words of amazement were flung my way. I was finally getting the attention I had so desperately craved and now all I wanted to do was run, run back to Tina, run back to the hotel, close the door behind me and bask in the silence and loneliness of the room.

A Dutch woman said I could stay at her house on my way through Europe, but before I could explain Amsterdam wasn't on my route, her husband squirmed and very unsubtly shook his head.

The conversation changed to dinner and I followed them up to a large banquet hall with a silver platter buffet on a white linen table that ran the length of the room. Dark meats in even darker sauces, multiple vegetables in various forms and a plethora of gout inducing desserts filled the posh dishes and platters. I went between Bill and his cronies and the buffet table a total of six times, each time my plate filled high. I ate quickly and quietly as if unsure when my next meal was coming, the table looked on in wonder yet I cared little. I was eating the food I could only dream of a week or so ago. It felt as though I had been released from some self-induced gulag.

I still hadn't calmed down from the intensity earlier in the evening and found myself getting short and defensive with almost everyone. Aside from Bill the other drivers gave me nothing more than intentional looks in the other direction, their faces held a judgment on my appearance.

Their conversations focused around their wallets, "Well I had to have a part flown in on my plane" and "I couldn't decide which one of my fleet to bring so I employed a professional race crew to drive the other one." It wouldn't have taken much for me to sock one clean in the jaw, a misplaced laugh or downward look would be enough. I'd get thrown out from my free dinner but I would feel good, justified knowing that regardless how much money you had in your pockets it did nothing when a fist hit your jaw.

I knew early on that money doesn't make you rich, it's your actions and character that matter. I started working at the age twelve delivering newspapers, then onto cleaning dishes at thirteen. I've had a job ever since, everything I have was from graft, hard graft, literally shovelling shit at times. Growing up in Oxford the probability of you running into some trust fund kid or silver spoon brat was high, I hated being around them. 'So what does your father do?' was a favourite question of theirs. I'd always answer with a,

'He puts the glue on post-it notes' or 'He went to jail when I was a kid.' Just so I could sit and bask in the confused and scared expressions. What bearing did my dad's job have on me? I was me and he was him. Judge me on my actions not what I was born into. It infuriated me then and it did now, the swagger some of these people moved with gave them the same self-entitled air that those kids had back home. Even if I had the loafers and expensive watch you could see in my eyes that I was a proud working class kid, nothing was going to change that.

    The food, on the other hand, was rich, opulent and deeply satisfying. I was now having to force feed myself because my body was so full. With my fill achieved I sat there resting on the back of the chair listening to conversations, unable to find a point on where to join. Even though their hardships were similar and easily assimilated I realised their stories weren't mine. My stories were between my ears, with Tina and the open sky. I soon knew I had to move on and keep my own story moving. These people weren't as bad and ruthless as my mind had concluded they were just focused on their own adventure. I thanked Bill for the food and handed back my Mechanic's pass. It was now night and the cold air hit my eyes bringing me back to earth.

    I went and sat on the cold wet floor next to Tina, hunkered down by the engine. I pulled out a piece of bread from my pocket that I took from the banquet hall and pulled it apart with my fingers. I ate a piece then tossed a piece to a pigeon that was on the ground in front of me. It was late for both us to be outside but the cold air felt beautiful as it fell down the back of my neck into my jacket.

I didn't say anything to Tina, just gave her a pat as I swung my leg over the saddle and started the engine. I roared the engine to full throttle piercing the silent night with her guttural scream. I pulled up to the main road, lifted my chin to the sky and let out the largest howl my lungs could muster. Again and again, roaring the throttle, I was a wild fucking animal and I liked it that way.

Over the next few days, I saw Bill and the other guys at a couple of rest stops and a few small towns yet I kept to myself exchanging a simple thumbs up and or an open palm as I once again assumed my place with the horizon. In amongst the worms and dirt I trundled ever closer to Europe.

SLOVENIA

Slovenia was not at western European standards but it was a definite upgrade from Ukraine. My expectations were held with Belgium, Germany and France so I had planned Slovenia in a rush, allowing several tourist websites to dictate my choices on where to stay. For the first night, I had decided to stay in a national park that was the home to the Skocjan Caves. I had seen photos making them look like something out of *Lord of the Rings*.

I entered down a long winding road through thick forest, I thought back to the Tiaga and the endless Birch. Here the trees were denser yet thinner, growing in erratic directions with impenetrable foliage. I slowed and removed my helmet, and pottered on at ten miles an hour for the remainder of the trail leading to the park.

I finally arrived at a quaint hotel nestled in the hillside. I knew I was spoiling myself staying in hotels but deep down I was tired, tired to the bone and back again. I hadn't stopped moving for ages and the miles were taking their toll along with the loneliness. I was greatly homesick, growing like a fast tide with every day that passed.

Home was with Libby and to some extent with my family in England. I knew that sometime in the not so distant future I was going to need to make a decision and commit, but for now I was feeling excited about the ideas of what lay ahead, what our lives together would look like, the children we would one day have, the house, we would raise them in, the adventures we would go on, the love we would share, the relationship that would grow between me and our children as I got old and their lives grew into their own. All of this now seemed like a release rather than the chains I'd previously put on these thoughts.

The roads were simple and straight forward in Slovenia and I wasn't being hassled by anyone. Petrol stations were now marked on road signs and the borders were easy to navigate so I had very little distractions to keep my mind focused, like the setting sun the inevitable tiredness kept closing in.

I kept dreaming of driving an old truck down to the beach next to the town that Libby and I would one day live in. I'd surf at sunrise and bring home fish to cook with the kids. I'd have a company doing good in the world, working with bright inspiring people. All of these thoughts and more started to become a huge source of energy for me. I had every reason to keep on rolling, not a single one to stop.

CZECH REPUBLIC

My day was short for the miles I had to ride, so I was making a detour to the Sedlec Ossuary. During the twelfth century, a monk had returned from the Holy Land with soil from Golgotha, which was where archeologists think Jesus was crucified. The Church took on a holy reputation of legendary proportions and had people coming from all around asking to be buried there, soon the church was overwhelmed with forty thousand bodies to be buried, so the monks took to cleaning and displaying all the bones from the bodies, a chandelier made from pelvises and femurs, a coat of arms made from everything else and stacks upon stacks of skulls towering twenty feet high.

I was starting to feel more conscious about my appearance, a week or so ago I would have been content stark naked in the town square, yet now the oil torn shirt and trousers I had relied on for the last two months brought too much attention. I made my way to a few shops to avert the wondering eyes, walking into the store I felt like Julia Roberts in *Pretty Woman*. My jeans were covered in oil and dirt, my shirt also, and my laces had snapped some time ago which I'd replaced with the reflective paracord I carried for a makeshift washing line. A few shops and few more Euros later, I was fresh and mean, walking with an ease like Axl Rose on stage. I had asked for my old clothes to be put in shopping bags, the clerk asked if I wanted her to get rid of them for me instead. I looked at them sitting there at the bottom of the bag all sad, I just couldn't bring myself to say goodbye. I pushed the bag up under my arm, declined the offer and hit the streets.

I could readily connect to the Internet and was talking to Libby on a regular basis. I was missing her more and more but the ability to see her face on a nightly basis made things so much better. I had forgotten how beautifully delicate her face was and how filthy and funny her mouth could be. We had planned a trip to Paris once I was home, I couldn't wait to put on a clean shirt and wander the streets not thinking about my route. I smiled at the idea of holding her hand at dinner whilst we sipped on a light white wine. Both of us were fans of fresh summer wines, zippy and tart, it kept us feeling fresh as the night drew long. Red wine would send us both to sleep.

I had booked a room in a tiny boutique hotel in Saint-Germain-Des-Pres, an artsy neighbourhood with great restaurants. It was close to the Seine where I knew we would spend hours walking back and forth talking, laughing and discussing our future. Prague was similar to Paris with beautiful buildings and mysterious streets to disappear down, Libby would have loved to be here and get lost in the back streets and alleyways. The thought of holding her hand during an early morning walk was bending me out of shape, the best I could do was grab a coffee.

I found a small smoky place with pit faced locals, each keeping to themselves dragging out the cigarettes and coffee. I turned a small chair and faced the world moving by in front of me, sometimes I felt as if I didn't have any depth at all but out in front of me was the cosmos, all these lives spinning freely in the great beyond. I knew not a single person yet I felt totally at home. I was yet to understand why anyone would want to root themselves anywhere for an extended period of time, if you had your loved ones by your side it seemed that anywhere could be home.

GERMANY

Road conditions could make or break a day, whilst the worst roads at the time would make me want to be anywhere else, yet in hindsight they almost seemed enjoyable, like a tough training session. I slogged and slogged and got through it, and looking back gave me a sense of nostalgia, almost to the point of wanting, wanting to be stood between the deep gravel, thick mud, loose sand or huge potholes. Germany was renowned for its beautiful roads and autobahn yet now I was on it, I had a whole other problem, I was too slow. Anytime I'd need to overtake I'd encounter some German branded car going at terminal velocity, making me feel like I was trying to tread water on the edge of Niagara Falls. They had outlawed flashing headlights at cars ahead to move out of the way yet this seemed to be a selectable law, as too often would I see a 911 or an M3 race up, flash and expect me to side hop into the small gap between two eighteen wheelers.

 I was staying with Claus; a friend I'd made in Mongolia. He and his buddy rode beautiful KTM's out in the Gobi Desert for a blast before coming back the following summer to ride to Magadan. I took the exit for Claus' hometown and was off the autobahn and back onto country roads, dry, beautifully smooth twisties.

 I arrived in a small quintessential German cul-de-sac, which sat perched on the side of the gentle green valley. As I pulled up a woman walked over to me from a few houses over.

'Hi,' she said, in perfect English.

'Hello.' Curious whether my number plate gave me away or that she knew who I was.

'Claus won't be home for a while,' she explained. 'He had an emergency at one of his clients, so you're going to come over and have dinner with us.'

What a strange and wonderful world this was, yet another stranger was looking after me. So off I trotted, bags in hand into this woman's home. Not long after sitting down with a large glass of water, her two young sons came home from school. They were a bit confused yet after a little explanation we were in full swing. The youngest was eager to practice and hone his English, more specifically his impressive collection of swear words, that seemed not to bother his mum. Soon we were in full vulgar conversation using as many words as we could at one another... tits, arse, fuck to you, bollocks to that idea, it's shit, well he is a prick, yes I know, a real wanker.

Soon attention was drawn by one of the only things that can create laser focus from a teenage boy; food. It was dinner time! Lucky for me she was used to feeding boys and the quantities in which they ate. The three of us sat there chomping, laughing and talking the evening away. I was having so much fun with my surrogate family I forgot I was there to see Claus, and when he stood there in the doorway it took a while to register who he was. Soon hugs and laughs spread to Claus as he pulled a seat to the table.

Claus explained we would head into the old town and attend the annual beer festival that marvellously coincided with my visit.

The old town was straight from a nursery rhyme, steep polished cobbled streets with wood framed houses leaning out over me. All the twisted and dark alleyways, paths and roads lit with ornate lamps led to a grand church upon a small yet steep hill top. Me, Claus and Joachim, a huge man in every direction and Claus' best friend, waited in the dark cool air for a hunchback or a vampire to leap between the bell towers but nothing came, so we had no other reason than to go get a beer. A beer is what we got, along with whiskey, vodka, Jaeger, gluhwein and lots more beers. Soon the cobbles were a hindrance, glistened with the cold night air and spillage. We skated, stumbled and laughed our way around the festival from tent to tent. Deep into the night we roared, cheering and smashing our steiners at any and every occasion.

Morning rolled around, along with the cold sweats that only a deep hangover can muster. All the moisture was on my skin rather than in my mouth which was as arid as the desert. Claus somehow looked as chipper and perky as he always did. Shuddering between deep sleep and belly burps I slowly snacked on the bacon and eggs that were plopped before me. Today, I had planned to head for the Nürburgring Ring for a hot lap, yet the mere idea of turning the key almost drew me to tears. Claus poured a solid splash of whisky into my coffee bringing a small amount of humanity back to my bones. If any day was a day to choose to be soft, today was that day. I decided to switch plans and make a beeline for my day's final destination in Brussels. I was happy to leave the hangover and fast drivers behind.

BELGIUM

My last night in Europe I decided to go all out, it was the last of my money, leaving me with nothing but pennies. It was a four-star hotel right in the middle of Brussels. I felt like celebrating, I had come so far I simply could not comprehend it. My sense of worth that was growing bigger by the day was consuming me, oozing out of every pore. I stopped frequently at petrol stations and roadside cafes as I had all of three hours to ride, three measly hours!

How I would wince and cry as a kid when we had to drive four hours to go to the campsite for our annual weeklong camping trip. I would sit there and just look at my dad from the rear seat and admire how strong he was, how tough he must be to stay focused and awake for so long in the dead of night, especially when my mum and sister would pass out for the majority of the journey. His toughness would keep me awake. I didn't like the idea of him driving alone whilst everyone slept, so I would sit there under the mound of pillows that made up the back seat, sweating due to the three feet deep foam that encapsulated me and my sister, transfixing my eyes on the road ahead, just like my dad was doing.

In Siberia I rode for ten to twelve hours a day just chugging along, now I had to find things to fill my time. I had seen enough monuments and relics to last a lifetime so I wasted a whole hour thinking of the best way to waste time. One way would be to complete my on-bike yoga routine, which I developed to stretch out my hips whilst riding, another great way to waste time I would try and drink a whole bottle of water with my helmet on. I even tried removing my jacket and putting it back on again whilst on the bike.

Then it hit me, like seeing a gorgeous woman, it was quite simply the most beautiful thought I'd had in days… I needed an ice cold pint and maybe some mussels and chips or "Moules Frites" as these odd Belgium bastards called them. I gunned the throttle, hunkered down on the tank and beelined for my four-star castle. I made it in half the time.

Brussels was a wealthy city and it showed. Most of all encapsulated in the facade of my hotel, it really was like a castle and the curb in front was cornered off by thick red rope held between gold posts, flags of multiple countries flew at a forty-five-degree angle from the hotel face. In the middle of the flags sat the gently lit hotel name made up of hundreds of delicate showbiz bulbs.

I dived Tina through the ropes and screeched to a stop in front of the hotel. The doorman, unfazed, walked to the edge of the kerb, put his hands behind his back and started talking to me.

'Huh?' I questioned as I unstrapped my bags.

'Sorry sir but we are fully booked tonight,' he repeated, this time in English.

Looking down at my trousers we both noted the state I was in, my exhaust had melted completely through my right trouser leg allowing you to see my knee and calf underneath. What remained of the rest of my riding suit had gone from a black to a kind of musky brown and green, heaven only knows what I smelt like. I marvelled at the fact that I was close to resembling the bums I had seen in Paris so many years ago. We both looked back up at each other, his face held a polite smile that silently said: "Now fuck off". I had already removed my large roll bag and it was now in my hands, which I tossed at him in a high arched throw, he caught it, startled.

'Lucky I reserved a room then,' I stated. 'I'll be back for the rest in a bit old boy, first I need a pint.'

I flicked my eyebrows up and down and walked past him as he looked on with a mixture of anger and disbelief. I strolled straight to the front desk.

'Where is the bar?' I inquired.

"Well, sir we have the lounge bar which is a mix of ..."

'Ok, which is closest?'

'There is one over there, sir,' she said, pointing to an archway at the back of the lobby.

'Thank you,' I said tipping an imaginary hat.

I found a red leather stool and perched myself at the end of a small brass bar.

'One beer please, whichever is coldest.'

I sat there smiling, wondering how long the doorman would wait till he came and found me. The beads of condensation ran down the pompous glass my beer had been poured into. I was able to get through two beers or roughly six minutes of time before he came and found me.

'I'm sorry sir but you are going to have to move your motorcycle,' his voice now strained.

'Understood.' I nodded and made my way back outside.

I stowed my bike in the underground parking lot and headed for my room. As I made my way up in the lift and entered my room another beautiful thought hit me, a twilight thought of drinking another ice cold beer. This idea was then taken to a whole new level when I realized I had a bloody balcony in my room, all to myself. What could be better I thought than drinking an ice cold beer, stark naked on my hotel balcony the day before I arrived home on my solo motorcycle expedition around the world?

Room service couldn't move fast enough, I paced the room waiting for the beer. Where was it? My lips were drying out, my heart raced. Had anyone had a heart attack from beer deprivation? Maybe I was about to be the first. I was about to collapse from dehydration, I had to focus. I flung the balcony doors open and assessed which spot was best to stand in. Clearly the right-hand side, it would mean I was facing the sun and a hundred or so windows to which I could entertain with my well-travelled pale and skinny body, albeit my tanned wrists and neck from the hot days in Kazakhstan, giving me a look of a reject chip-n-dale.

A knock at the door. I extended an arm around the door patting for the beer bottles. I was afraid of exposing my already naked body or showing too much of a view into my room giving away my master plan. I thanked the faceless waiter behind the door with a few euros, put the lock and latch on and marched straight to the balcony. There I stood pale and naked as a newborn baby lamb holding two Heinekens as the sun shone.

'Life is grand,' I said out loud and without further ado, I let rip the biggest howl I could muster. I was felt simply untouchable.

The night drew in, with my new clothes on that I'd picked up in Ukraine I pranced in an inebriated state into town. The doorman was now smiling at me without the smallest clue that I was the gipsy from earlier. What a difference water and a hand through the hair can make. Tonight was my last on this large stretch of land that had begun all the way back in Vladivostok.

This huge piece of dirt that I was leaving behind, that so many people called home. Most of the people that lived between Vladivostok and Brussels were hidden from each other, by the curve of the earth. Tonight was the last time I'd see the sun set over the land that had taken me to new heights only to see how far I could fall, then allow me to pick myself back up. I wanted to talk to no one, so to let the beauty of this world wash over me for one last time. I knew soon I would be in the arms of Libby, growing a business in New York, and whatever mayhem was coming my way, but tonight was simply about silent love.

I found a small restaurant that was washed out from too many summers. Painted in blue and white it was small and forgotten by the majority of the passers-by and set back under a heavily grown ivy arch. I chose a rickety old table hidden back in the dark behind two open French doors that looked out through the dark green canopy over the narrow square. I got a cheap bottle of white, a big pot of mussels, and some frites as I drank and ate the world away. "The words 'far away' had always a strange charm." someone once wrote. I'd been there now.

Across the square, over the small patch of green a young couple dressed in their evening best swooned and snapped at each other's lips. A tired eye business man walked quickly, his tie askew. Silently he moved, watching the ground with a tortured face, rushing to get home, to safety, to the sanctity. I sat there, holding, witnessing this secret of tranquillity and absolute beauty. No one knew that I had such a powerful key, like a secret weapon to topple an empire. Yet it was no use for me to swim around in these thoughts, the sun had now fully set, the couple kept at it, their hands shook with passion struggling to find where to go. They were bound to this bench, no other place would allow them to express themselves with such raw heat, they had no room to escape to, no home without scornful eyes. How could something so simple as young love be so universally confusing?

As a species we have an overwhelming and destructive power to oversimplify, break things down to their ones, twos and threes and base our whole life on simple easy steps, missing the intricate spider web of connections to the world around us that make it what it is. Like when we slash woodland and remove top soil, kill the worms and wonder why the regrowth is weak and half what it was, so to spend my life spinning in the euphoria created by my wanderings over the last few months would have me miss life's complexity. I needed to forget all that I had seen, bury myself in the next world that opened itself to me, taking care of the characters, dirt and sky that would be part of it, listen for the sparks, smoke, hum and waves of tomorrow. I just had to keep moving, a lesson that the earth, the sun, the planets, and everything in between knew all too well.

I was tired, beat, and with the sun disappearing behind the broad and rich buildings, I tucked the last of my money under my espresso saucer and headed back through the streets. No grander thoughts came my way, just get up, strap the bags on and ride home.

FRANCE

Seagulls swam in circles on the summer thermals, they screamed and yelled at the ocean, they appeared black in the bright early morning sun. It was warm already, the breeze was forming, pushing gently against my chest as I rode towards the sea. Sand was being whisked up the banks, I could feel it hitting my throat like tiny drum beats, beating the notes of the sea.

I had changed my train crossing to an early departure, so there was no time to stop, no time to sit back and kick it in the dunes, no time to say hello, no time to say thank you. I was to ride and ride I did as fast I could go, roaring down the coastal path, the wind kept punching my side letting me know where I was.

There is nothing more beautifully brutish than the sea. She devours countries and valleys and now she was eating me. The sea reminded me I wasn't grand, I wasn't big, I wasn't the trade winds or the rolling Southern Ocean. I wasn't a sun flare or a mighty meteor in flight but I would show my teeth anyhow and show them I did with a giant howl. The sea and I laughed, what absurdity, like we had never left one another. Our conversations were the same, we both sat there in each other's company all the way to Calais.

The road to the port grew busy with a myriad of bikes from Japanese rockets, to the grand tourers, the old greats and everything in between. Where were they all heading?

I pulled through the boarding gates as an odd sod with a fat jaw and loose skin paid me no mind as I gave him my ticket and took my place in the lane, ready to board the big metal train that ran its belly under the English Channel and rose its big Leviathan head in Dover. Once on-board, we had to park at a forty-five-degree angle in the narrow carriage, packed in tight, like metal sardines. I was dirtier than all and decided to sit down out of the way, I soon moved as the fumes consumed my eyes, Tina was with her friends and sat content, murmuring with her pack caused by the cooling of the contracting metal.

"Where have you all come from?" I quizzed.

"Assen."

"Oh the GP, who won?"

"Rossi then Marquez."

He moved away.

"How was the MotoGP."

"Good."

They moved away.

He, then her, then them and then him, they all moved on, again I was back in the swing of nothing more than a simple ride.

I pushed my headphones in and laid flat on my bike, the slow jazz songs of the beat generation jingled and jangled and jangled some more, as the train slowly pulled away. I had made some notes in my book when I could finally feel it, the train was slowing. I checked my watch and we had been in motion for the right amount of time, it meant only one thing, we were in England.

I couldn't control my limbs, I was shaking, I didn't want to control myself. Yet we had to wait, it was hell. I wanted to see the sky over my home, the land that raised me, no other time in my life had I wanted to be back home so badly. I had spent the majority of my life running, to university, then London, then Boston, then New York. Finally, the large side doors swept back on the train, the daylight rushing in. I was home. I stood on my pegs bouncing the bike and howling, I was bursting with joy, twenty-six thousand kilometres, and I was in my final country. Tomorrow, after a brief stop in London, I'd be home!

We all straddled our bikes as the train came to a halt, it took forever to get out of the train. It was slow, people were faffing around and I was getting frustrated. I just wanted to be back, back on English soil and here I was only fifty feet away and some woman couldn't get her fat leg back over her bike. I took a breath, then another. Finally, we started moving, it was agony, we were moving at a snail's pace. My energy surged and soon I found myself on the dock, I was stood tall, dancing on my pegs, a man rode up and asked me to calm down.

'Never', I yelled back. 'Do you know how hard I've worked to get here?'

He looked perplexed. I gunned the throttle and blasted down the line, up the steep ramp looking for which way to turn. There it was: the motorway. It took time for my eyes to adjust to yet another new set of road signs and their layout, I knew them so well yet it was as if

I had never seen them at all. I was back on the right side of the road, it felt odd, unfamiliar. Next stop was Greenwich in London.

ENGLAND

I was now in a rush. I wanted to complete it and fast. Dover, London then Banbury. I passed Brands Hatch and was back in London, muscle memory or the subconscious took over. I was zipping through cars in central London when I felt a lurch and wiggle at the rear. I had clipped a lorry with one of my panniers. I totally forgot I had all this luggage on, I slowed down and calmed myself.

I headed towards the monument at the top of Greenwich Park, now a beautiful yet sticky tourist trap this once was a grand private hunting ground of some nobleman. There were deer still held in the north of the park, a reminder to the penned killing that took place here not so long ago. I came to a stop at the furthest most point, I grabbed my camera and walked to the beautiful lookout, down the hill over Greenwich, then onto the Thames to Canary Wharf. To the left stretched central London all with its beautiful sights. I wondered what it would have looked like before the Luftwaffe appeared. What would be different? Maybe I could go back even further and meet Scott as he learnt to sail and command at the Naval academy at the bottom of the hill, before embarking on the worst journey in the history of humankind. Such an exquisite tapestry of endeavour. Powerful and taken for granted technology stemmed from this small plot of land, once again my grand ideas of times past were overtaken with a need for a beer or two.

Tonight I would be staying with my brother James. We grew up together and ran to London as soon as we could. I switched into bike commuter mode and hazed the streets I knew so well, heading straight to his house. It was a real treat not looking at the map to get where I needed. I turned up his street in record time. I gave Tina thanks again for not kicking me when I was getting carried away. James opened the door and stood at the end of the garden path, I gave him a hug so big it picked him off the ground. We stood in silence as I unpacked and got changed, it was nice being around people you didn't need to fill in the silence. We walked the all too familiar streets to the pub I had wasted many summer days, soon we were sat on the heath outside the pub with our pale legs in full blaze sipping on an ice cold beer. Another James and Robin, friends from University, joined and a few others and soon I was back in time. I hadn't just ridden around the world, or even left London, we sat and laughed at the awfully awkward situations Clarkey seemed to get himself into with the women of this great city. His energetic voice squeaking with the fumbling and stumbling of the various bra straps and conversations.

The grass was still soft and in abundance, yet to be trampled by the summer mass migration of boozers and joggers. In England, summer is by no means guaranteed so when the sun shines and the temperature is slightly above freezing we come out of the woodwork, the hiding spots and the garden sheds. We assemble in the village pub garden or at the cricket or in the garden next to a BBQ.

We sat there with beers flowing freely and laughs growing longer and louder. The cold came in and we moved inside for food and yet more beer. This pub had been our "local" for the four years I lived in London, it was quintessential in every way. It was small, drab and old, the barman was grumpy as hell but the food was hot and the beer was cold. All day I kept saying how much I was fond of being back, but I really wasn't, the finish was still another eighty-six miles away, up the M40, just one more day.

I knew this deep down in my subconscious and it kept me on edge, never fully allowing myself to relax, because like the ninety-two days behind me I always knew there was more focus, more action, more movement needed and today was like no other. Yes I was in England, yes I was with my friends but they weren't strong enough to push the switch, the switch that says relax, it's all over!

I ordered some comfort food in the shape of a steak and kidney pie, it came with mash, gravy and peas, it was dense and honest. My friends made me feel safe and content, the small brass light fixture above our table was flickering, it had been there for years, probably longer than I had been around. The flickering bulb mesmerized me and I soon found myself visualizing the route home, the shortcuts I'd learnt over the years, the signs that I was getting close to home, like the third and final turn for Oxford, or the rolling woodland that always no matter how much I anticipated it would always just appear, stretching out, presenting Oxfordshire. I could feel my mind starting to wind up, my muscles shortened, I brought my feet into the base of the seat, I straightened my spine and palms began to sweat.

'James,' I whispered.

'Yes, mate.'

'I'm knackered; I might have to call it quits soon.'

'Sure thing, I have work tomorrow, let's just grab a film at home.'

'Perfect.'

HOME

I stood there, fastening my bags as Tina's engine slowly grew with speed, breaking through the cold stiffness. Soon she hit the resting rpm my ear had become so in tune to. I knew if she was running rich or lean or low on fuel from her burble.

I roared to the bottom of the road, turned and waved to James, and gunned it north. I zipped through traffic, bullying my way to the motorway. Soon I found myself tucked on the tank. I was pushing Tina hard to keep the pace. She strained and struggled, the motorway signs took forever to come, the mile markers I was so used to, thirty-two, sixteen then ten then the three chevrons for my junction. I waited and waited, I could hear the seconds ticking past, then without realising it I was heading down over the flyover, pass the industrial estate, left onto the main road into town then right. I hit the apex perfectly, completely on the wrong side of the road, as I righted the bike the tear ducts opened. I could see my home. I could do no more than let the tears roll and roll they did, along with big full body gasps for air. I had done it, just me and Tina, around the world.

I had turned into the small street where I grew up and ahead of me, my sister was stood barefoot yelling down the driveway.

'He's here, he's here,' she screamed.

My dad, mum and niece came out to see me, it took everything I had to stay upright, I stayed on the bike, both feet on the floor, crying my eyes out.

'What's wrong?' my dad asked.

'I've done it Dad, I've actually done it.'

Tears welled in his eyes, mum was already in tears, we were all crying apart from my niece, with the sobering simplicity of a child's mind, she couldn't realise why we were sobbing in the street. Uncle Paul had ridden home before, so what's all the commotion?

I calmed myself down and squatted down by Tina, I thanked her for everything. As I turned to carry my kit into the house, I noticed a bed sheet hanging from my old bedroom window, on it was written "Welcome Home Paul - Boston to Banbury".

Right there and then it was clear, there simply is no love like home. Whether it was the large boots, the layers of dirt or something that had grown inside of me, the hallway to the kitchen felt narrower and lower. I rounded my shoulders to fit and ended up in the kitchen. My parents' home is one of the big loves of my mother's life, she tends to each nook and cranny with care and attention that anyone else would part on their own children. I had barely come to a stop before my mum spoke.

'You're not putting that in here,' she stated, pointing at my bags.

I smiled, noting that nothing has changed, so we hauled everything out the back onto the decking. We all looked around waiting for someone to ask or me to start answering, answering all those questions they all had. Within seconds Mum was pulling out my smelly clothes, it was incomprehensible to her how anyone could get so dirty and if they did why on earth they would stay that way.

'We should just throw this all away!' she exclaimed, pinching at arm's length my jeans and shirt.

'Never, they're trophies from the road, there are over 400 species of dead bugs on the jeans alone.' I declared through grinning teeth.

'Ok fine, but I am washing them on their own, I don't want them touching any of my washing. I'll probably have to do a whole other wash to clean the machine.' She grumbled as she walked inside.

Her face held a look of loving frustration, but deep down we both knew she loved the drama that I brought through the doors, from dirty clothes to emptying the fridge.

With everything splayed out on the ground, I marvelled at all the kit. The pieces that had saved my ass like the cable ties, gaffer tape and the pieces that were still in their original wrappings like the spare chain and a sprocket, the water purification tablets and the elaborate first aid kit.

I must have been hugged a thousand times since arriving home. I was most excited to see my nephew and niece, however for them, Lego was far more important than their smelly uncle Paul. I was able to grab a quick hug and a kiss but back to playing they went, through all the chaos of being home, I felt completely lost, what the hell was I going to do now?

I had no plan, no itinerary, no road signs to look for, it was scary and nauseating. I felt a huge sense of impatience. The next item on the list was Libby who was to fly out and meet me in London and from there we would head over to Paris, but that was two weeks away. What was I going to do for that amount of time? I could cover about seven thousand kilometres in that time, now I was home back in this simple town, with the unchanging streets, the same faces and the static sky overhead. The urge that had me wanting to run when I was sixteen was now pounding in my ears again, maybe a soak in the bath and good sleep might calm me down. I went upstairs to find Mum and Dad had changed the bathroom and got rid of the bath, so I sat in the shower letting the water get heavy, falling down on my shoulders and hair, my heart rate dropped and a tiredness set in.

I awoke early the next day, no one else was awake so I crept downstairs and sat down on the couch watching cycling on Sky. So many mornings as a kid I would get up early on a weekend and watch Transworld Sport with my dad, waiting for the action sports segment or some weird and wonderful sport I'd never heard of. Why were there so many channels now? I used to be able to waste hours flicking between channels, now I felt fidgety. Was I becoming something that I had only read about in books, was I becoming productive?

I found myself emptying the washing machine, I moved Tina into the back garden and onto her centre stand, I decided she was never to be cleaned. I made a mental note to emphasize this to my dad, who like a nervous tick would clean all the cars and bikes every week, regardless if they were the slightest bit dirty. I stowed the panniers in the shed and walked back to the house. With everything stowed and my clothes now clean, I had very little to do other than realise that it was over.

EPILOGUE

I should start this section off stating this is just an incoherent list of thoughts that the trip inspired me to have, maybe the fact they are incoherent and sporadic is a sign of the after effect.

As I sit and write this, my life has infinitely changed. I am now living in New York with my wife, Libby. I am working with two guys and a host of others growing an amazing company, managing an ever expanding team. On my bike it was merely me, I had Tina but she was impervious to misdirected ideals or haphazard comments that I would let fly. Now, many people look my way for support and guidance, leadership and love. This is infinitely harder than dodging knife fights in Siberia or staring down a rifle barrel in a Kazakh jail. I always said to myself and others that I was born to wander.

Was this trip escapism from responsibility or responsibly escaping out of the world I did not belong? I am a little lost in the melancholy of manhood. I often find myself daydreaming, being back with Tina driving on a lone road in Kazakhstan, Mongolia or Russia, just breathing the air of the empty horizon, it calms the wolf that just wants to howl.

It took nearly six months after the trip for me to realise what I had accomplished, I had bear claws in my pockets and scars on my legs, my heart was singing a loud soulful song that I hope will never go quietly. So many people said I didn't have the expertise to accomplish something like this but I did, so can you, so could anyone.

Throughout the whole trip, I did not see another Triumph Scrambler, but we had made it, she was heavy, slow and cumbersome as an adventure bike but she had looked after me for the majority of the time. Yeah, she had thrown me to the ground and pitched me and burnt me but she never grumbled, she never complained, when she cried oil she was easily fixed and on we went, when she snapped she was welded.

There was a quiet sense of something lost, I didn't know whether it was just the sound of the trip being over or if I'd left a piece of me out there, part of my psyche, something I would never be able to replace. If I had known this before leaving I would have scared myself half to death, I was so afraid to let me be me, as a dynamic state, a fluctuating wave, society seemed transfixed on the idea of the defined human, an unwavering completeness, whilst my traits would always be there the wisdom I could learn could overcome any ill-gotten word that came into my thoughts.

So when people argue over can people change? The answer the expedition gave to me on this question was yes and no, we have things about us that will never change, let's call these things traits, such as I have come to realize I will always get defensive or upset when someone says something derogative to me. I am not one of those people that chuckles as a knee jerk reaction, most of the time I just want to sock them, yet getting to know myself so well whilst I was hidden inside my helmet helped me come to that conclusion that this is simply what happens, neither good or bad but just happens, knowing what I do in those situations then enabled me to be able to adjust myself before I spoke or reacted, so whilst my reaction wasn't going to change, my response was.

There is an afterlife, it is not some other realm or place above the clouds or outer space, but why would you want that any way? Our world under and all around us is so damn beautiful! The best form of an amazing afterlife that I reckon we can hope for exists in the minds of our loved ones that we leave behind. I can think so happily of great times with both my grandfathers, from going to air shows, watching him nurse sick birds back to health in the pocket of his cardigan to the late night mental quizzes he would set. There in those thoughts they both exist, a series of synapses and electric pulses create these hugely vivid images and mental movies that elicit all the love and response I had when they were around, so in my eyes, they still exist, with me, within my thoughts, well after their funerals had ended. We can directly affect the strength of those memories by how strongly we love and care for those people dear to us whilst we are here.

So I really need to try and not be a dick!

I now belonged to Libby and the family we would create, we talked on where we would decide to settle down, we talked about California or South America. We want the city but space and ocean and mountains. We don't want much.

I could talk at length about the lessons and changes that had taken place, I had seen more of the world than most people would see in a lifetime and yet I know I have barely scratched the surface. I could state that the more I saw the less I knew and the more I just had to let it all go, yes that was true, I set out to find myself only to realize I was there all along and you don't find yourself, you make yourself, into the person you want to be, through hard work, scaring yourself, and never giving up.

USE THIS SPACE TO PLAN YOUR OWN ADVENTURE.

DON'T THINK, JUST DO!

www.ingramcontent.com/pod-product-compliance
Lightning Source LLC
Chambersburg PA
CBHW022101090426
42743CB00008B/675